50 THREATS
TO A GOOD
GOVERNMENT
EMPLOYEE

Avoid mistakes that hinder
your ability to get the
most out of your
government service

SEBEKE JEFFERSON

ISBN: 978-218-88345-4

Cover design by: Nanjar Tri Mukti

Interior design by: Sebeke Jefferson, with design assistance from Mama Daniel

Printed in the United States of America.

This book is a work of nonfiction. The experiences, observations, and viewpoints expressed herein reflect the author's personal perspectives developed over decades of government service. Names, situations, and examples have been generalized where appropriate to preserve privacy and intent.

For information, permissions, or inquiries, contact:

Sebeke Jefferson

www.50threats.com | 50threats@gmail.com

Dedication

To my grandfather, Mr. Ronald Hardy, the man who first planted the seed of public service on my life.

I can still hear your voice saying, "Beke, you need to get you a good government job, boy." At the time, I laughed it off, thinking you were just talking about job security and benefits. But as the years went on, I came to realize you understood something far greater than the true meaning of service.

What I once thought was simple advice about stability turned out to be a calling about purpose. You knew that serving in government wasn't just about earning a living, it was about making a difference, standing for something bigger than myself, and ensuring that the people around me could depend on that very same service.

Your words stayed with me, Granddaddy, and they grew into a lifelong commitment to serve. Every accomplishment, every lesson, and every challenge in my career traces back to that moment from your influence and your wisdom.

I love you; I miss you, and I thank you, Sir. You started it all.

Table of Contents

1

Failure to Understand What You Want to Give to Government Service and What You Want From It

This is very important, and not everyone realizes it before entering government employment. Many people pursue a "government job" without fully understanding what they are stepping into. However, entering public service without a clear sense of purpose or without expectations about how you want to contribute can create long-term problems.

A lack of purpose can lead to stagnation, disengagement from the mission, and eventually resentment toward the work itself. It does not feel good as a taxpayer to seek government services and encounter someone who appears uninterested in serving the public. Likewise, it does not feel good to provide government services in a position you do not believe in or feel connected to.

This is why it is critical to first understand what you want to give to government service, rather than focusing only on what you want to receive from it. When the mindset becomes "what are they doing for me" instead of "how can I improve the service," the balance is lost. That does not mean government employees should accept poor working conditions or lack support. On the contrary, government workers deserve positive work environments, fair benefits, and the resources needed to do their jobs well.

Many government positions are represented by labor unions whose role is to advocate for employees. That advocacy is important. At the same time, it remains our responsibility as public servants to provide high-quality service with care and professionalism. The relationship between employee support and public service should be balanced, not one-sided.

An important question to ask is: "*What do I want to be fulfilled by in my work*"? For example, if you are processing driver's licenses for the state but have a strong interest in instruction, you may find greater fulfillment administering driving tests instead. It is common for applicants to enter government service with only a limited understanding of the work they have applied for. It can take time to determine where you fit best.

This is why government employees should continuously orient themselves both during the hiring process and throughout their careers toward how they serve. Government careers often allow movement between departments or job classifications over time, providing opportunities to realign with your strengths and interests.

Am I serving in the right place in government? How do I know when it's time to change, or if I should change at all? These questions arise frequently in public service careers. Often, the answers begin with understanding what you are good at and how well you know your job. Do you understand not only your role, but how it connects to others around you? Learning the full scope of your position can reveal future opportunities and clarify your path.

For example, a grounds worker responsible for lawn maintenance across multiple school sites may also have an interest in planning and coordination. By fully understanding the work section and seeking additional training in scheduling or logistics, that employee becomes more immersed in the mission. This improves performance and shifts the mindset from simply completing assigned tasks to actively managing and improving the work.

Learning more about your role can involve arriving to work early to review productivity goals, seeking mentorship from coworkers who excel in their positions, and consistently practicing your craft to improve efficiency. Regular self-evaluation of strengths and weaknesses helps establish a clear understanding of where you are in your service. Doing your best work where you are is essential before deciding where you want to go.

Government service should not be solely about what you give, even though that is a central component of public duty. Government workers should also gain fulfillment from their work. The work should be engaging, meaningful, and connected to a mission that invites participation. This includes having a healthy work environment, reasonable benefits, and leadership that recognizes employees as individuals not machines.

People bring their full lives into their work, including personal challenges and lived experiences that can affect their ability to serve. Acknowledging this reality is part of building sustainable public service.

This topic is listed this threat first because many people attempt to reinvigorate their government careers without first understanding what they want to give to public service or what they need to gain from it in return. This understanding may come quickly or take years to develop. What matters most is a continued commitment to seeking that answer.

2

Merging the Negative Social Culture with Your Work Ethic

I f you ask staff members from different sections of government what a negative social culture is, you may receive many different answers. Ultimately, however, your ability to cultivate and maintain a positive work ethic toward the service you provide is what matters most. Not everyone approaches government work in the same way. There are supervisors and managers who actively encourage employees to understand their service more deeply and to look for ways to improve it.

Serving within a government section or office that produces work as a group can be challenging. Some sections divide responsibilities among several people, with the pace of work determined collectively rather than directly by a supervisor. While the work must be completed, the group may calculate how long tasks will take within a given timeframe. For example, you may have worked in a section for several years when employees' complete tasks individually. You take pride in completing assignments efficiently and consistently look for ways to improve productivity.

Now imagine transferring to a new section of government. In this section, there is an established social structure among employees that influences how work is approached. The group collectively determines how long tasks should take, often based on social relationships rather than efficiency. This may feel unfamiliar, especially when you believe tasks could be completed more effectively. When you attempt to contribute ideas to improve productivity, you encounter resistance. You may even be encouraged to become socially connected to the group before offering suggestions.

In this situation, the challenge becomes learning how to work effectively within a group whose motivation model differs from your own. Adapting to a new environment does not mean abandoning your work ethic. It means understanding how to engage constructively without allowing negative social dynamics to undermine your standards or the mission of the service.

Working in a setting that fosters a negative social culture does not require you to adopt that culture. Social culture within a workplace can influence productivity, morale, and professional growth. This threat is not intended to discourage social interaction. Government agencies are made up of people who work closely together, including colleagues from adjacent sections. Some coworkers become friends, while others remain strictly professional contacts.

Problems arise when professional relationships begin to negatively affect work ethic. When social alignment becomes more important than service outcomes, productivity suffers. The key question is whether these dynamics influence you positively or negatively.

Government employees will always encounter coworkers and sections with differing views on how work should be done. That is normal. What matters is understanding your role, your standards, and your responsibility to the mission. Over the course of a government career, approaches to service may change based on personal growth, career goals, and evolving motivations.

Progression in government service depends on maintaining a work ethic that supports the mission, whether working individually or as part of a group. Allowing social culture to distract from service goals can lead directly to the issues described in this threat. In many instances, social work cultures can become the priority over the mission itself. What people think of you or whether they like you becomes more important than the service being provided. Existing within this dynamic requires discipline, clarity, and intention. Boundaries must be established early to protect both your work ethic and the mission you serve.

3

Diminishing the Scope of the Service That Your Position Provides

M any government positions come with formal job descriptions. These descriptions establish expectations and outline basic responsibilities. Some positions are newly created, while others have existed for many years. In either case, job descriptions often focus on specific tasks. This does not mean the government is failing in how positions are structured. It may simply mean that a position has not yet reached its full potential.

Some believe that expanding or refining a position is solely the responsibility of managers or human resources professionals. While those roles are important, no one understands a position more thoroughly than the individual who performs the work every day. In many instances, positions evolve from the ground up as employees gain experience and insight. When employees help shape how a position functions in practice, the role itself can become more effective and valuable to the organization.

There is also a widely held belief that government employees should perform only what is explicitly required and not challenge the scope of their position. For some, this mindset is acceptable. They are comfortable working within established parameters and accept both the efficient and inefficient aspects of the role. However, when dissatisfaction exists alongside a refusal to improve or adapt to the position, conflict can arise. Being unhappy with inefficiencies while choosing not to address them limits both personal growth and service quality.

This threat does not suggest that all government positions should be dictated from the ground up. Nor does it imply that employees should assume the roles of management or human resources. Instead, it challenges the idea that government employees should work within a position without fully understanding it or considering how it might function more effectively. Everyone has a role to play. Those who create positions do their part, and those who work within them do theirs. The question is how often employees focus on what does not work rather than exploring where improvements are possible.

Consider an example involving administrative support in a fire department. One responsibility of the position is processing payments for office supplies. Another section of the department determines which supplies are ordered. Over time, you recognize that it would be more efficient for your section to manage its own supply decisions, since you already handle the purchasing process. This does not mean management made a poor decision. It may simply indicate that older practices have not kept pace with current workflows. Management cannot observe every operational detail, which creates opportunities for employees to provide insight and suggest improvements.

Not everyone knows how to improve the position they hold. Some employees feel frustrated because they believe the scope of their role limits progress. They understand their duties but avoid exploring areas where improvements could be made. This is not necessarily due to a lack of motivation. Often, it results from not fully understanding how the position functions beyond its written description. Job postings and evaluations describe responsibilities, but lived experience reveals what actually drives productivity and outcomes.

For this reason, it is critical to understand every aspect of your position. This requires regularly revisiting the job description, identifying what works well, and recognizing what does not. This understanding develops over time and cannot be achieved in a few weeks. While performing the duties of a position is necessary, continuously learning how the role operates allows for meaningful improvement.

When aspects of a position are ineffective, opportunities often exist to communicate concerns and ideas to management. Choosing to do nothing and allowing the scope of a position to shrink unnecessarily limits both the employee and the service being provided. This is why diminishing the scope of your role becomes a threat to being an effective government employee.

4

Refusal to Personally Invest in Your Own Career

"If they are not paying for it, I'm not doing it." What does this statement really mean? Is this threat suggesting that government employees should personally fund training in place of an agency's responsibility? On the contrary, this threat presents an alternative way of viewing self-investment. It speaks about taking partial ownership of where your career is headed and how you get there.

Not all government agencies have the funding to provide additional continuing education, and those that do often have limited availability or selection processes. Whether training opportunities are abundant or scarce can determine whether a government career moves forward or remains stagnant. As referenced in other threats within this book, rejecting training opportunities altogether can contribute to stagnation over time.

There is a difference between taking advantage of available training and actively seeking training on your own. Consider an example in which you work for a local transit administration. You express interest in an agency-wide training program focused on subway rail safety, but you are not selected. Later, you learn that the training was offered to employees based on job title, experience, tenure, and merit. This training aligns directly with your long-term career goals, so you research the program independently and discover that it costs $300.

At this point, several options present themselves. You could wait for the agency to offer the training again. You could become discouraged and abandon the effort altogether. You could complain to your supervisor, suggesting unfairness, even though the training was allocated appropriately based on operational need. Or you could choose to invest in the training yourself. Would that be foolish? Would it be a waste of money?

There is no single correct answer. Each choice leads to different outcomes, both positive and negative, and those outcomes will vary depending on the individual and their career goals. In this example, the training is critical to your future aspirations. As many government employees know, not all training is guaranteed, and many of us adjust our career timelines based on availability rather than intention.

Whether this reality is viewed as good or bad is a matter of perspective. Later in this book, particularly in Not Taking Ownership of Your Government Career, the importance of proactively managing your career path is explored further. One way to do this is by seeking training independently when it supports your long-term goals.

Before entering government service, many applicants invest in themselves by obtaining degrees, certifications, or specialized training. Once hired, that mindset often shifts. We may begin to rely solely on our agencies to provide development opportunities. While many agencies do offer training, these opportunities are frequently limited, preassigned, or influenced by factors beyond individual interest. Even when training is advertised broadly, participants may already be determined.

This reality forces an important question: If this training were required for a position you truly wanted, and you had the means to obtain it yourself, would you do so? Depending on your answer, action may be necessary.

This threat does not suggest that government employees should personally fund all professional development. Rather, it encourages a broader view of self-investment. Some employees bring degrees earned through years of education, while others carry trade certifications or extensive continuing education. Government service evolves due to many factors, including changes in leadership, technology, policy, funding, and public need. Even when job titles remain the same, the nature of the work often changes.

As government service changes, so must those who provide it. Aspirations to grow or serve in new ways can be limited by a lack of qualifications. Training departments cannot always meet every need. While this threat does not address attitudes of frustration or resignation, it does challenge employees to consider an alternative approach. For those open to growth, investing in your own career can produce meaningful results. Waiting solely on agency-provided training places the pace of your career in someone else's hands. Taking ownership of that pace is one way to actively shape your future in government service.

5

Failure to Take On Service Challenges

Government service can be repetitive, but it can also be constantly changing. In either case, many of us eventually reach a point where we have mastered our work. We understand the systems, know what is expected, and develop methods that allow us to complete tasks efficiently. This threat addresses what happens after that point is reached.

Once the work is mastered, different approaches begin to emerge. Some choose to remain comfortable with what they know, while others look for ways to improve or expand the service. There is a thin line between these two approaches. In some situations, an "if it is not broken, do not fix it" mindset can be appropriate.

Stability and consistency have value. However, government service does not exist in a vacuum. Public needs change, leadership changes, and expectations evolve.

Conflict can arise when employees have different views on whether improvement is necessary. Some may see no reason to alter the pace or scope of their work, while others feel a responsibility to adapt and improve. This becomes a threat when employees recognize problems or inefficiencies but resist making any effort to address them.

Consider an example involving a local health and human services office. Your section is responsible for administering service programs approved by the agency. For years, leadership rarely introduced new initiatives, allowing the office to provide the same services with little change. A newly elected official appoints an active administrator who introduces additional service programs. Suddenly, your section must adapt.

Within the office, different perspectives emerge. One approach is to continue operating as before, distributing services at the same pace and limiting outreach. Another approach is to develop information sessions and outreach efforts to ensure the public is aware of the expanded services. Choosing not to improve service delivery, simply to preserve a comfortable routine, may benefit employees in the short term but does not serve the public.

If the administration observes that services are not improving or adapting, responsibility may be reassigned to another section, leaving your office with reduced duties. When this happens, frustration often follows. Yet it is difficult to expect growth, relevance, or recognition when no effort is made to improve or adapt the work.

This threat does not suggest that every government employee must constantly push for change or expansion. Not all services require the same level of adaptation. However, it does speak to those who desire improvement in their offices or agencies without being willing to improve the work that supports that progress. Government work should not be overwhelming or unmanageable, but at its core, it exists to serve the public as effectively as possible.

Refusing to take on service challenges ultimately reflects in the quality of service provided. If the work does not challenge us, it is unlikely to challenge or improve the service itself. While not every position will change dramatically, recognizing when growth or adaptation is needed can shape both a career and the services delivered. If an employee is satisfied with their current contribution and sees no need for improvement, this threat may not apply. However, expecting better outcomes without changing one's approach often leads to disappointment.

6

Taking On More Than You Can Manage

Having ideas and taking on tasks in government service is a good thing. Initiative helps agencies move forward and keeps services evolving. However, with every idea and additional responsibility, there is a point where enthusiasm can turn into overload. Dedicated employees often take on too much at once in an effort to prove their worth, stay busy, or make a difference. The risk is that by doing so, you may end up working constantly without truly completing anything of value.

Ideas alone are not enough. If none of them are fully developed or executed, they lose their impact. Staying busy is not the same as being productive. Government service rewards results, not activity.

Taking on multiple projects without a clear plan may spread focus too thin. What begins as passion for progress can quickly turn into frustration when deadlines are missed and outcomes remain unclear.

Knowing your limits is just as important as showing initiative. Honesty with yourself about what you can realistically manage is critical. Every task you accept deserves proper attention and a clear plan for completion. Without that structure, even the best intentions result in unfinished work. The goal is not to do everything; the goal is to do what matters and to do it well.

Before agreeing to take on a new task, take the time to define your objectives, timeline, and the steps required to complete it. Government service is rooted in accountability. Incomplete work reflects not only on the individual, but on the team and the mission as a whole. When too many projects are left unfinished, the public does not see effort, they see a failure to deliver.

Taking on too much can also affect credibility. Supervisors and coworkers notice patterns. When someone repeatedly starts projects but fails to finish them, trust begins to erode, regardless of good intentions. A strong government employee balances enthusiasm with discipline, ensuring that each responsibility adds real value to the service being provided.

Vision is important, but without structure, vision becomes chaos. Completing one project with excellence will always mean more than starting several that never reach completion. Being strategic with your energy matters. Finishing what you start and knowing when to say no protects both your effectiveness and your integrity.

True professionalism in government is not measured by how much you take on, but by how well you complete what you accept. Managing your workload with purpose strengthens your reputation, reduces burnout, and delivers results that matter. Focused service is effective service, and that is what the public deserves.

7

Not Taking Ownership of Your Government Service

One of the greatest threats to being an effective government employee is failing to take ownership of your government service. Many employees come to work each day focused only on completing assigned tasks and going home. When service is viewed as just a job rather than a responsibility, growth becomes limited and the deeper purpose of the position is lost.

Taking ownership means understanding that every action reflects your character, your work ethic, and your commitment to service. It requires more than waiting for direction. Ownership involves recognizing what needs to be done and taking initiative to do it well. When you adopt this mindset, you move from simply following instructions to actively contributing. Leadership begins to show in how you approach challenges, solve problems, and deliver results.

Understanding and embodying your agency's mission is a critical part of ownership. Every government department exists for a reason, and that reason extends beyond paperwork, reports, or checklists. Government work is about serving people. When you take the time to understand how your role supports the broader mission, your work gains meaning and direction. Seeing yourself as part of something larger strengthens your connection to the service you provide.

Government employment should not be viewed solely as a position or title. It is a form of public trust. Public service demands accountability, integrity, and care. When you approach your role as service to others, pride naturally follows. Quality matters more, decisions are made with intention, and your work reflects the responsibility placed in you by the public.

Ownership distinguishes those who do the minimum from those who bring purpose to their work. It builds credibility, strengthens commitment, and earns respect from coworkers and leadership alike. More importantly, it gives your career depth beyond routine tasks.

Your government career gains meaning when you recognize that your position matters not because of authority or rank, but because of the impact you make. Every document processed, every citizen assisted, and every responsibility fulfilled contributes to the greater good. Ownership shifts the focus from earning a paycheck to serving a purpose.

Pride in service, intentional effort, and awareness of your role in government are essential. Government functions because individuals show up committed to fairness, accountability, and responsibility. When you fully take ownership of your government service, you not only protect your own career, but you help strengthen public trust. That is what true service looks like, and that is how meaningful professional legacies are built.

8

Staying Too Comfortable Within Your Position

One of the easiest traps for government employees to fall into is comfort. Many government jobs offer stability, security, and routine. Over time, however, that same routine can lead to complacency. When you remain too comfortable within your position, growth slows. Learning stops. Potential goes unrealized.

Government careers are often built for the long haul rather than short-term gain. Over a span of twenty or thirty years, it becomes easy to settle into patterns that feel safe and predictable. What feels comfortable today, however, can become stagnated tomorrow. A strong government employee learns to balance comfort with challenge. Growth rarely occurs in ease; it happens when you step into unfamiliar territory and push beyond what you already know.

When you stop challenging yourself, stagnation follows. The work may feel easier, but your skill set begins to narrow. Taking on new responsibilities, even small ones, keeps your thinking sharp and your value strong. Growth does not require overwhelming yourself. It requires intentional stretching. Volunteering for new projects, learning unfamiliar processes, or contributing outside your routine are opportunities for development.

One effective way to keep your career moving forward is to set goals to learn new skills or transition into different internal positions every five to seven years. Each transition exposes you to new systems, new colleagues, and new approaches to service. Over time, this creates a well-rounded foundation of experience. That depth of knowledge strengthens your contribution and enhances your credibility.

If you choose to promote or pursue a new role, you will compete with others who bring varied experiences and perspectives. The broader your background, the stronger your position becomes. Should you eventually transition into the private sector, the experience gained through government service carries lasting value. Leadership, adaptability, policy awareness, and problem-solving skills translate far beyond public service.

Comfort may feel safe, but it does not lead to fulfillment. Periodically reminding yourself that growth is still possible keeps your career alive. Government service offers countless opportunities for development, but only if you are willing to step forward. Challenge yourself intentionally, because comfort alone does not produce excellence.

A strong government employee never stops learning and never stops growing. Comfort is temporary, but growth has lasting impact. Each time you move beyond what is familiar, you strengthen your confidence, skills, and sense of purpose. Do not allow routine to define your career. Let progress define it. When your service concludes, the true reward will be knowing that every stage of your career contributed to becoming a stronger, wiser, and more effective public servant.

9

Interfering in Management's Failures Toward Your Work

This threat is a common experience for many government employees, especially those who have worked in the same position for several years. Over time, we learn what works well in our roles and what does not. Government experiences supervisory turnover just like other fields, but the difference is that turnover among working staff is often much slower. Some employees are promoted quickly, others transfer to different sections, while many remain in the same section for most of their careers. Those who develop a deep understanding of their work often experience a wide range of management styles. In many cases, managers and supervisors may not fully understand the technical aspects of the sections they oversee. Even with management degrees or prior supervisory experience, this knowledge can fall short in a new office or operational environment.

For example, consider working in the supply section of a police department. The position was once staffed by a civilian and later reassigned to a sworn officer. After years in the role, you understand what works best for government service and what does not. A new supervisor is assigned, having transferred from managing patrol officers to supervising civilian staff. The supervisor applies patrol-based management practices to your section, creating unnecessary difficulty. When you attempt to explain why these approaches are ineffective, your concerns are dismissed.

At this point, frustration sets in. Do you disengage and provide minimal effort? Do you attempt to transfer out of the section? Or do you sit back and allow the supervisor's initiatives to fail so you can later say that you warned them? Situations like this create significant frustration. Often, supervisors do not know what they do not know, and this can lead to micromanagement or decisions based on assumptions rather than operational reality. Problems arise when working staff possess more technical knowledge than their supervisors. This dynamic can contribute to one of government's ongoing challenges: the loss of talent due to managerial disconnect.

In a scene from the film *The Tuskegee Airmen*, Lawrence Fishburne plays Hannibal Lee, a newly graduated pilot who sees his first assigned aircraft with his name painted on it. He remarks that he has never had his own plane before. The crew chief,

Tank, responds by saying that the plane is not actually his, but that his name was added so he would believe it was. The point of this exchange is not ownership but understanding. Those who operate the aircraft know it intimately. Similarly, while managers and supervisors' direct operations, it is the working staff who understand the job at its most detailed level. As discussed in Not Taking Ownership of Your Government Service, those who perform the work daily carry a form of ownership that cannot be replicated through titles alone.

This is why it is important not to allow frustration to dictate how we respond to managerial shortcomings. While it is difficult, ground-level government employees must recognize that management also has a learning curve. Unlike operational staff, managers often learn from the outside in, relying on education and prior experience rather than daily execution. This creates an opportunity for working staff to help bridge that gap. As discussed in leading upward is sometimes necessary. Sharing insights, experiences, and solutions from a ground-level perspective can help supervisors make better decisions, even when they are reluctant to acknowledge their own gaps in understanding.

There will be times when supervisors refuse to learn from those they supervise. In those situations, progress may come through trial and error. While it can be frustrating to witness mistakes that could have been avoided, the goal should never be to watch management fail. Instead, the focus should be on preparing solutions in advance and helping correct issues once they become visible. This approach shifts frustration into purpose.

When managers make decisions that lead to predictable problems, documenting those outcomes and offering constructive solutions turns failure into a teaching opportunity. While constantly correcting poor decisions can be exhausting, it can also influence long-term improvement. Trust grows when supervisors see that their staff are invested in success rather than conflict. Helping management understand what they do not yet see strengthens the mission. In this way, interfering with management failure is not about control, but about commitment to service, professionalism, and the success of the agency as a whole.

10

Practicing Emotional Intelligence With the Ups and Downs of Your Service

Working in government can be frustrating. Many factors contribute to this, ranging from political shifts to internal management challenges. Newly elected leaders may introduce new priorities, policies, and expectations that change the direction of your work. At times, those changes may not make sense to the people responsible for carrying out the service. You may find yourself working under new directors, managers, or supervisors whose leadership style you do not believe in. In some cases, you may encounter leadership that creates a toxic environment, making daily work more stressful than it needs to be. Government service is full of ups and downs. It is a career shaped by change, and change does not always happen smoothly. One year may bring strong leadership and clarity, while the next brings confusion, poor communication, and conflict between departments. Some agencies struggle to work together until they are forced to, and when teamwork only exists under pressure, failure often follows. These experiences can wear on even the most dedicated public servant.

Many aspects of government service will test your emotions. Being emotional about your work is not a weakness. In many cases, it simply means that you care. What matters most is how those emotions are managed. Allowing frustration, anger, or disappointment to dictate your actions can damage your professionalism, your reputation, and your long-term career. Emotional intelligence begins with recognizing how you feel and making a conscious effort to separate those feelings from your behavior, so the mission remains the priority.

Your agency, its leaders, politicians, and coworkers should never control your emotions. You control them. While frustration may be justified, professionalism is always required. Emotional intelligence is knowing when to speak, when to pause, and when to act. It allows you to remain steady and effective even when your environment feels unstable. It is the skill that keeps you grounded when everything around you feels uncertain.

There will be times when you need to step back and refocus. That is appropriate and necessary. However, the mission must continue. Emotional intelligence may mean temporarily stepping away from a task to regain clarity without abandoning responsibility. It reflects maturity, discipline, and self-awareness. This ability separates those who simply work in government from those who lead within it.

Remaining emotionally intelligent is not optional in government service. It is essential. It protects your professionalism, your peace of mind, and your purpose. The strongest government employees are not those who never feel frustration, but those who know how to manage it and channel it into improvement, perseverance, and action. When you master your emotions, you strengthen your service.

Emotional intelligence is what separates good employees from great public servants. It is the quiet strength that allows you to maintain integrity when conditions are difficult. When you control your emotions, you protect your career and your credibility. Let professionalism guide your actions and let your service rise above every challenge. Calm, discipline, and self-awareness are the traits that define true public service.

11

Failure to Take Up for Yourself in Workplace Mobbing

B eing targeted by management or groups of coworkers is one of the most damaging experiences a government employee can face. You work hard, follow policy, and believe in the mission of public service, only to have those who should support you use authority, procedure, and workplace culture to isolate or discredit you. It is a lonely and confusing place to be, where your efforts go unnoticed, your voice is dismissed, and your reputation is quietly undermined.

Workplace mobbing in government often occurs in silence. It may stem from personal bias, jealousy, fear of competence, or exclusion from a social clique. Some employees are targeted for being highly capable, others for speaking honestly, and some simply for not fitting into an informal power structure. Regardless of the reason, mobbing distracts from the mission of government service. It erodes morale, weakens teamwork, and replaces service with fear.

Being in this situation can be frightening. Power imbalances are real, and management may hide behind policy or hierarchy to justify harmful behavior. Yet no government system should protect mistreatment or silence those who serve with integrity. Toxic workplace cultures can thrive when authority is used to enable predatory behavior rather than stop it. Taking up for yourself does not require hostility or disrespect. It requires professionalism, clarity, and self-respect.

The first step in protecting yourself is establishing clear boundaries around how you expect to be treated. Be intentional about what behaviors you will and will not tolerate. If certain dynamics interfere with your ability to serve, you are not obligated to participate in them. Serving the mission does not require adopting unhealthy social alignment or remaining silent in the face of mistreatment.

Operate in truth. Do not exaggerate your experience, but do not minimize it either. Document events, communications, and patterns that demonstrate unfair treatment. These records matter. They protect your credibility, clarify timelines, and provide grounding if formal review becomes necessary. Acting truthfully preserves your integrity even when others attempt to distort the narrative.

You do not have to endure this alone. Support may come from trusted coworkers, union representatives, counselors, or therapists familiar with workplace trauma. Government employees also have access to formal complaint processes, including internal reviews and Equal Employment Opportunity channels. While outcomes are not always immediate or favorable, choosing to act affirms that you will not quietly accept mistreatment. Those who engage in mobbing often reveal themselves over time.

Taking up for yourself does not make you difficult. It makes you courageous. The goal is not retaliation, but protection of your dignity and your right to work without fear. When one person stands in truth, it often gives others the courage to do the same.

While this threat focuses on the individual responsibility to protect oneself, later chapters examine the broader organizational damage caused when workplace mobbing is allowed to exist unchecked. As explored in Threat 30, Existing in Workplace Mobbing, silence does not only harm individuals, it weakens agencies, destroys trust, and ultimately undermines the mission of public service.

Standing your ground with integrity restores your sense of control and professionalism. Your worth, skill, and purpose are not defined by how others treat you. Government needs employees who will not be bullied into silence, people who continue to serve with honesty and strength despite adversity. Standing in truth is both your defense and your anchor. It protects not only your career, but your peace of mind.

12

Having an Affinity for Government Failure

After experiencing workplace mobbing or unfair treatment, it is understandable that some government employees lose faith in their agency. When you have been excluded, disrespected, or ignored by the very organization you have given your best to, it can leave a lasting sense of disappointment. Over time, that disappointment can harden into resentment toward the entire system.

These feelings are normal. Many dedicated employees reach moments where they think, "This place doesn't deserve my best." While those emotions are valid, allowing them to define your outlook is dangerous. A negative experience, or even a series of them, should not be allowed to poison your commitment to the mission. Government is far larger than the individuals who fail within it.

Even when leadership falls short, the need for service remains. The public still depends on the work being done. Whether issuing licenses, maintaining public safety, responding to emergencies, or managing essential resources, the mission does not stop. Your role continues to matter, even when morale is low or management appears disconnected. Government service is not solely about who is in charge. It is about what the agency exists to do and who it serves.

The failures of a few leaders should never convince you to want the mission itself to fail. Leadership changes. Administrators retire, new directors arrive, and priorities shift over time. What remains constant is the responsibility to serve the public with competence and care. When frustration leads employees to disengage or quietly root for failure, the people most affected are not managers, but the citizens who rely on those services.

You should always want your agency to succeed, even when the environment is imperfect. Government service is not about personal pride; it is about collective responsibility. Many public servants are not only employees, but also recipients of the very services they provide. When government fails, it affects everyone, including those who work within it. Remaining committed, even after personal setbacks, is a mark of true professionalism.

Having an affinity for government failure does not correct injustice. It deepens it. The most effective response to poor leadership, unfair systems, or toxic workplace cultures is to continue doing your job with integrity. Each time you uphold the mission despite disappointment, you help restore confidence in public service. You become an example of what government should be accountable, resilient, and focused on the people.

Never allow bitterness to replace purpose. Your professionalism, patience, and consistency are what keep the system functioning when others lose sight of its importance. Good employees who continue to do good work will always outlast bad management. When you refuse to root for failure, you stand for what government is meant to represent service, stability, and the belief that improvement is always possible.

13

Personal Agenda vs. Service Tasks

Having a personal identity connected to government service is not a bad thing. In fact, it often drives the best work from dedicated public servants. Passion and belief in the mission can inspire higher performance, stronger commitment, and more meaningful contributions. The danger arises when that passion shifts into a personal agenda, when decisions are made not for the benefit of the public, but for personal gain, recognition, or convenience.

Every government employee should ask one critical question related to this threat: How do my decisions benefit the public I serve? The answer reveals whether motives are aligned with the mission. Choices, actions, and recommendations must always serve the greater good, not ego, not social standing, and not personal ambition.

At times, decision-makers within government attempt to gain support or build favor by promising faster results or cutting corners to meet short-term objectives. When decisions are driven by personal interest, whether for power, influence, or advancement, the foundation of public trust is weakened. Government exists to serve the public, not the personalities operating within it.

Taxpayers do not simply fund salaries; they fund outcomes. Every decision made in government carries both financial and ethical weight. When personal agendas take priority over fairness, efficiency, and honesty, the consequences are borne by the citizens who depend on those services. Trust erodes, and confidence in government diminishes.

Before making any decision, it is essential to check your motives. Ask whether emotions, loyalties, or frustrations are influencing your judgment. Public service requires discipline, the ability to separate personal interest from professional responsibility. It takes integrity to make decisions that benefit the public even when they do not benefit you personally. That discipline defines a trustworthy government employee.

If personal benefit outweighs service in your decision-making, you should not be guiding outcomes in government. Leadership is not about control; it is about responsibility. Service is not about self-interest; it is about stewardship. Each time you choose the mission over personal agenda, you reinforce the principles government is meant to uphold: integrity, fairness, andaccountability.

Public service is a privilege. When personal purpose aligns with the mission, progress follows. When it does not, trust is damaged and effectiveness declines. Keep your focus where it belongs, on the service, the people, and the responsibility entrusted to you. That is how true government professionals rise above self-interest and serve with honor.

14

Friendships Over Service

C amaraderie within government can motivate us to do our best work. Many of us collaborate with coworkers, share ideas, and experiment with new service models. These relationships often develop through training, daily operations, and shared responsibilities. But what about relationships formed through special interests outside of work? What about friendships that existed before gaining government employment?

Some of us serve in communities where we grew up. It is common to work alongside people we knew long before entering government service. Many government employees are social by nature, especially in small or closely connected agencies. We lean on fellow employees to discuss service successes, frustrations, and challenges. These relationships can be healthy and supportive, but they can also create ethical tension when not properly managed.

Many government employees serve other government employees rather than the general public directly. Quartermasters, vehicle mechanics, payroll processors, and administrative specialists all provide internal services that keep agencies functioning. The question becomes this: does the quality of service change depending on who is being served? Do we go the extra mile for coworkers we like while doing the bare minimum for those we do not?

This threat is not meant to suggest that friendships in government are wrong. Many of us will naturally form close relationships at work. The threat arises when those friendships influence who receives quality service and who does not.

For example, imagine you are a quartermaster in a government maintenance shop. Employees across the agency rely on you for uniforms and equipment. Over time, you form friendships with many of them. Some of those relationships extend beyond work to fishing trips or golf outings. At the same time, there are employees you do not connect with or may even dislike.

When your friends request equipment or replacements, do you prioritize them? Do you respond faster or provide more flexibility than you would for someone you are not close with? Is this simply human nature, or does it cross a professional boundary?

The public does not expect to receive better service because of personal relationships. No one believes they should be extra friendly to a firefighter to receive help during an emergency or to a mail carrier to ensure their mail is delivered. Service is expected to be fair, consistent, and impartial. The same expectation applies within government agencies when serving fellow employees.

This threat extends beyond peer relationships. Many government employees eventually promote into supervisory, managerial, or director roles. With promotion often comes influence over staffing decisions. While many agencies rely on structured promotion systems and union agreements, there are still opportunities for leaders to place individuals into key positions.

At that point, motivation matters. Are decisions being made because someone is the best fit for the role, or because they are close friends? While those two factors may occasionally overlap, this threat focuses on situations where personal loyalty overrides professional judgment. If you know someone else is better suited for a position but choose a friend instead, service integrity is compromised.

Every government employee should ask themselves this question: can I clearly separate personal relationships from professional responsibility? Some friendships enhance teamwork, while others hinder productivity. There are also situations where friendships deteriorate, creating tension that spills into the workplace. When fear of damaging a personal relationship prevents you from doing what is best for the mission, service suffers.

This threat is not about discouraging friendships in government. It is about recognizing when those friendships begin to influence service decisions. When personal relationships dictate how effort is applied, government service becomes a social exercise rather than a public responsibility.

Different perspectives are welcome, and not every situation will look the same. However, when a particular approach consistently produces negative outcomes, refusing to adjust it will likely lead to the same result. The ability to draw clear boundaries between friendship and service is essential to maintaining professionalism, fairness, and trust in government work.

15

Fame and Glory Seeking

Why are you doing what you do in government? That's a question every public servant should ask: Why are you doing what you do in government? That is a question every public servant should ask from time to time. This idea has appeared in earlier chapters, but it deserves focused attention here. If your motivation for service is recognition, a follow-up question becomes necessary: can you truly stay focused on the mission with that intention? In many cases, the answer is uncertain.

There is nothing wrong with being proud of your accomplishments. Recognition for a job well done is a natural and healthy part of professional life. However, there is an important difference between being recognized and "seeking glory". When the pursuit of praise or visibility becomes the goal, attention shifts away from the public good and toward self-interest. Even when this shift begins subtly, it can slowly erode the purpose of public service.

Public service is not a stage for performance; it is a platform for responsibility. When success becomes centered on personal image or reputation, the collective effort behind the work is overlooked. Government functions through teamwork, coordination, and shared accountability. A true professional does not need to announce their contributions. Their value is demonstrated through consistency, reliability, and results.

The desire for personal glory can also create division within the workplace. When one individual seeks constant recognition, trust among colleagues can weaken. Collaboration may suffer as others hesitate to share ideas or contributions, fearing they will be overshadowed. In this way, fame-seeking behavior distracts from the mission and damages workplace culture.

Government service is built on consistency, not celebrity. Many of the most effective leaders work quietly behind the scenes. They manage details, solve problems, and ensure continuity without seeking attention. While they may never receive public praise, they earn something more lasting: respect. Their credibility grows because their focus remains on service, not visibility.

It is also important to remember that recognition in government is temporary. Administrations change, priorities shift, and praise fades. What endures is your reputation, your record of doing the right thing even when no one is watching.

Seeking attention may bring short-term visibility, but serving with humility creates lasting value.

The strongest government employees do not chase recognition; they earn it through their work. When your focus remains on the mission, acknowledgment follows naturally. Let the quality of your service define your legacy, not the attention it attracts. Fame fades, but integrity endures. When you work for the mission instead of the mirror, you serve with purpose, and that is what makes you truly effective.

16

Distracting Yourself with Social Culture

Being social while serving in government is a good thing. Over a twenty- or thirty-year career, building relationships can create teamwork, strengthen collaboration, and establish a professional network that lasts a lifetime. The connections formed through shared work experiences can make the job more enjoyable and, at times, support career growth. There is nothing wrong with being social at work. In fact, healthy interaction can be motivating and beneficial.

The problem arises when government service begins to morph into a Social CAS or a conditional access system where those who are socially connected have access to positive work environments.

When social culture becomes the focus over the work, it distracts from the mission. The purpose of being at work is to serve, to provide, and to fulfill responsibilities that the public depends on. Of course, government staff can and should have a social aspect to the people we work with. However, when conversations, alliances, and social systems begin to dominate time and attention, the quality of service inevitably suffers.

Social culture can become a distraction when who we like or don't like in our government offices and sections become toxic. It often doesn't look harmful at first, but when this occurs the dynamics can change. The effects can show up as government staff transferring out to escape the toxicity. The staff members who thrive in toxic work environments may be able to control the work environment of an entire office. This dynamic can overall create a negative work environment through informal leadership. The real issue emerges when government staff become more concerned with discontent, bias, maintaining popularity, or protecting social standing than prioritizing the service. When social circles influence who receives information, support, or fairness, the workplace stops being professional and starts becoming completely something else.

The goal should always be balanced. Healthy workplace relationships should support the mission, not slow it down. Social interaction should strengthen collaboration rather than divide it. Being approachable and friendly does not require losing focus. It requires knowing how to communicate with professionalism, respect, and purpose.

Government service must always be about the work first. The public does not see the internal social dynamics of an agency.

They see the results. When social distractions take priority over duty, the mission is compromised. Friendships and humor have their place, but they should never come before service.

The strongest government employees understand how to manage both. They build relationships without sacrificing professionalism. They support coworkers without joining unproductive cliques. They remain focused on the mission even when the surrounding social culture drifts off course. Being respected for your work will always last longer than being liked for your mere presence.

When you keep your focus on the mission, you set the standard for what government service should look like: committed, dependable, and professional. Let your work speak louder than your social circle. Serve with purpose, connect with integrity, and remember that while friendships may change, the mission must always remain the priority.

17

Involving Your Government Service with Politics

Politics has a rightful place in our society. It ensures that collective interests are represented, public resources are managed, and the overall direction of government is shaped by elected leadership. Political leadership decides what needs to be done, but government employees decide how it gets done. When those two roles blend in the wrong way, problems begin to surface.

When politics becomes intertwined with the work of ground-level government operators, the integrity of the service is put at risk. Government workers are expected to carry out the mission objectively, without favoritism and without political bias. When personal political beliefs or political pressure begin to influence decisions, public trust erodes. The service becomes less about fairness and more about ideology, and that damages confidence in government as a whole.

A clear and firm boundary must exist between political leadership and operational management. Elected officials may establish policy, but it is the responsibility of the workforce to implement that policy fairly and professionally. This separation keeps the service focused on execution rather than agenda. Once the mission becomes politicized, government loses balance, credibility, and consistency.

It is also important for government employees to understand that political loyalty is not the same as professional duty. You may personally support a particular leader, party, or ideology, and that is your right as a citizen. However, when you step into your professional role, your responsibility shifts to the mission and to the public. The people you serve represent every political belief, and all deserve equal treatment.

Blending politics with public service can also divide the workplace itself. When political discussions, favoritism, or alliances dominate an office, the environment becomes distracted and strained. Morale declines, productivity suffers, and the mission fades into the background. The focus shifts from serving the public to navigating internal political dynamics.

Professional government employees remain neutral. They carry out their duties with fairness, integrity, and respect for process. They may not always agree with the policies they are asked to implement, but they understand that their role is to serve the system, not reshape it according to personal beliefs. True service is not about political gain; it is about stability, consistency, and trust.

Your mission in government is not to promote politics. It is to provide service. The public should feel confident that when they walk into a government office, they will be treated fairly regardless of who they voted for or what they believe. When you keep politics separate from service, you protect the credibility of your agency and the foundation of public trust. That is how government remains fair, functional, and worthy of the people it serves.

18

Judging Coworkers with Different Work Ethics Than You

overnment staff are not the same. We come from different backgrounds, bring different skills, and approach our work in different ways. Some of us move quickly and prefer to finish tasks early, while others take more time to focus on details. Neither approach is automatically right or wrong. The strength of government service comes from combining these differences to accomplish the mission together.

One of the most common sources of workplace tension is judgment. Comparing how others work to how we work can quickly become destructive. When we begin to believe our way is the only right way, we lose perspective. Judging coworkers who work differently creates division, resentment, and poor communication. It also prevents us from recognizing contributions that may not be immediately visible.

Not everyone approaches tasks with the same pace, style, or energy. Some employees excel at organization, others at analysis, and others at execution. When these differences are respected, they strengthen the team. When they are criticized, they weaken it. A strong government employee learns what coworkers do well and finds ways to partner with those strengths rather than focusing on perceived shortcomings.

Teamwork in government is built on collaboration, not comparison. It is easy to point out what others do not do well, but it takes maturity and leadership to recognize what they contribute. Every role matters, and every position supports the mission in some way. When we choose understanding over criticism, the work environment becomes healthier, and the service itself becomes more effective.

There will always be coworkers who operate differently than you do. Some may not share your sense of urgency or your approach to problem solving, but that does not mean they lack commitment. As long as the mission is being fulfilled, differences in work style are not a weakness. They are an asset. Learning to respect those differences will make you a better coworker and, over time, a better leader.

A good government employee lifts others rather than tearing them down. Instead of judging, guide. Instead of comparing, collaborate. The public depends on all of us working together toward shared outcomes. When we focus on collective success rather than personal standards, we build trust, improve performance, and strengthen the culture of service that government depends on.

19

Inability to Complete Service Tasks Before Going to the Next

A common issue among government employees is the habit of moving on to new tasks before finishing the ones already in progress. In a busy work environment, it is easy to become distracted by new assignments, incoming requests, or last-minute priorities. However, when tasks are left incomplete, even with good intentions, confusion, delays, and frustration follow. Others depend on your work, and unfinished tasks disrupt the entire chain of service.

Taking on multiple assignments at once may feel productive, but it often has the opposite effect. Each unfinished task becomes an open responsibility that weakens efficiency and accountability. Government work depends on structured processes, and each process relies on the one before it being completed properly. When that sequence is broken, the quality-of-service declines and problems compound.

Completion is just as important as effort. Anyone can begin a task, but it takes discipline, focus, and responsibility to see it through to the end. A partially completed task is still unfinished work, and in government service, unfinished work can delay outcomes for the public and create additional work for coworkers.

Before moving on to the next assignment, it is critical to review what is already in progress. Ask yourself whether all requirements have been met, whether documentation is complete, and whether follow-ups have been handled. These details matter. Ignoring them often leads to mistakes that must be corrected later, costing more time and resources.

The most effective government employees value consistency. They do not rush from task to task simply to appear busy. Instead, they work with intention and completion in mind. This approach builds trust with coworkers and leadership and demonstrates reliability in both routine and high-pressure situations.

Trying to manage too many unfinished tasks at once can make even a strong worker appear disorganized. Focus on one task, complete it fully, and then move forward. That discipline builds credibility, reduces stress, and ensures your work truly contributes to the mission. In government service, completing what you start is a clear reflection of professionalism, and professionalism is what earns lasting respect.

20

Accepting Stagnancy Within Your Service

O ne of the greatest dangers in a long government career is accepting stagnancy. It rarely happens overnight. Instead, it develops slowly, often disguised as routine. You come to work, complete the same tasks, and go home. Over time, you stop asking questions, stop looking for ways to improve, and stop challenging yourself. When this happens, your service becomes motionless.

Government work often rewards stability, but stability should never become stillness. There is a difference between being dependable and being stuck. When stagnancy is accepted, professional growth slows and motivation fades. The belief that "this is how it has always been done" begins to replace curiosity and innovation. That mindset limits not only your progress, but also the agency's ability to adapt and improve.

There are always opportunities to make work better. Every office, department, and division has room for improvement. Yet stagnancy causes those opportunities to be ignored. Instead of asking how the process can be improved, employees settle for what is familiar. In government service, "good enough" is rarely good enough for the public that depends on us.

Breaking free from stagnancy begins with self-awareness. Take time to evaluate your mindset and your work habits. When was the last time you learned a new skill, improved a process, or stepped outside of your comfort zone? If it has been a while, that awareness is your signal to act. Growth does not require reinventing the wheel. It requires staying engaged, curious, and committed to being better than you were before.

Leadership plays a role in encouraging growth, but individual responsibility matters just as much. Waiting for someone else to motivate you often leads to remaining stuck. The strongest government employees find ways to move forward even when growth is not formally encouraged. They invest in learning, seek new perspectives, and remain open to change.

Stagnancy does not affect only one person. It spreads quietly through teams, dulling creativity, lowering morale, and weakening productivity. When you choose to remain active, engaged, and eager to learn, you set an example that others notice. Positive momentum has a way of spreading just as easily as complacency.

Public service thrives on progress. Every improvement, no matter how small, strengthens trust between government and the people it serves. Do not allow your career to be defined by habit or comfort. Keep learning, keep contributing, and keep moving forward. The public deserves your best, and your best is never found in stagnancy.

21

Being Fearful of Management and Your Administration

C hange in government is constant. Whether it is a new director, a promoted supervisor, or a shift in administrative leadership, transitions are inevitable. With each change comes uncertainty, and for many government employees, the arrival of new management can create real anxiety. Familiar routines disappear, and new expectations, personalities, and priorities take their place.

Feeling uneasy during management changes is natural. You may question how new leaders will operate, whether your work will be valued, or if your position will be affected. Many of us have served under leaders who inspired confidence and others who created stress and confusion. The uncertainty between those experiences can spread tension throughout an entire department.

Mid- and upper-level management transitions often bring shifts in direction. Priorities change, policies are reexamined, and routines that once felt stable are suddenly questioned. Adjusting to these changes can be frustrating, especially when they occur frequently. However, adaptability is one of the most important skills in government service. The ability to adjust without losing focus is what allows good employees to remain effective through change.

Fear of new management can quietly limit your performance. It may cause you to hold back ideas, avoid communication, or assume that every change will lead to negative outcomes. Not all change is harmful. New leadership can bring fresh perspectives, improved systems, and opportunities for growth. Remaining professional, patient, and open-minded allows you to evaluate change based on results rather than fear.

When leadership turnover occurs, focus on what you can control: your performance, your attitude, and your professionalism. You do not have to immediately trust new management, but you should allow them the opportunity to lead. Just as employees adjust to new leaders, managers are often learning their roles under pressure. Many experience the same uncertainty they now oversee.

A new administration cannot take away your skills, experience, or dedication. Those belong to you. As long as you remain committed to the mission, your value does not depend on who holds authority. In government, leadership will change, but the mission endures. Strong employees outlast transitions by anchoring themselves to service rather than personality or politics.

Fear of management should never prevent you from doing your best work. Stay respectful, remain professional, and continue delivering consistent results. Over time, reliability earns respect from any leader, regardless of their style or background.

When change arrives, do not let anxiety control your actions. Let experience guide you. New leadership may alter direction, but it cannot change your purpose. Stay focused on the mission, and you will maintain balance no matter who occupies the top seat.

22

Ignoring the Opportunity to Lead Up to Supervisors

In government service, leadership does not only flow from the top down. While supervisors and managers are tasked with directing operations, the working staff often hold the deepest understanding of how the work actually gets done. Ignoring the opportunity to lead up to supervisors is a threat because it allows poor decisions, inefficiencies, and avoidable failures to take root. Those closest to the work often see problems long before they reach management's attention.

Leading up to management is not the same as dictating to management. It is not about undermining authority or overstepping roles. It is about educating supervisors through ground-level knowledge and daily operational experience. As discussed in earlier threats related to management challenges and change, such as Fear of Management and Your Administration and Interfering in Management's Failures Toward Your Work, employees on the front line often recognize what works and what does not before anyone else does.

Leading up includes proposing ideas, maintaining continuity of operations, and offering informed suggestions that support the mission. This may involve explaining why a particular process is inefficient, sharing observations about service delivery, or recommending adjustments based on real-world experience. These efforts are not acts of defiance; they are acts of responsibility. When done professionally and respectfully, they strengthen the organization rather than challenge it.

There will be times when management does not listen. This can be frustrating, especially when the consequences of inaction are obvious to those doing the work. However, this is not the moment to become disengaged or to quietly hope that leadership fails. As explored in Having an Affinity for Government Failure, wishing for failure only harms the mission and the public. Management missteps affect everyone, not just those in charge.

Opportunities often return. A decision that fails may create space for learning. A supervisor who once resisted feedback may later seek it out. When those moments come, the employee who remained professional, prepared, and solution-oriented is best positioned to help management help themselves. Leading up is not about winning an argument; it is about preserving the mission through patience, persistence, and integrity.

Government service works best when communication flows in all directions. Supervisors lead, but they also learn. Employees follow, but they also inform. When working staff ignore the opportunity to lead up, they surrender one of their most valuable contributions. When they embrace it, they help build stronger leadership, better decisions, and more effective service for the public.

23

Accepting "Dead End Service"

There are few things more limiting to a government career than accepting what can be called "dead-end service." This happens when an employee stops challenging themselves, stops learning, and becomes content with performing the same tasks year after year without seeking growth. It is an easy trap to fall into, especially in positions that offer routine, security, and familiarity. But when this mindset takes hold, we quietly give up on our own potential.

As discussed in earlier chapters such as Staying Too Comfortable Within Your Position and Accepting Stagnancy Within Your Service, there is a clear difference between being dependable and being stuck. Dependability means showing up consistently and performing your duties well. Being stuck means avoiding challenges out of fear, indifference, or complacency. Dead-end service is not created by the agency alone; it is created by an attitude that says, "This is all I will ever do."

Every government role, no matter how repetitive it may seem, has room for improvement. When employees stop looking for ways to refine their work, increase efficiency, or learn new approaches, the quality of service begins to decline. Government service relies on people who are willing to evolve, adapt, and take pride in improving how work gets done, even in roles that appear routine on the surface.

Choosing comfort over growth does not create stability; it leads to gradual decline. Over time, this mindset drains motivation and leaves employees disengaged and unfulfilled. When change inevitably arrives, those who have accepted dead-end service are often the least prepared to adapt. Confidence weakens when skills are not exercised and curiosity is abandoned.

A government career is a long journey, and those who finish strong are the ones who remain engaged throughout it. Growth does not always mean promotion or title changes. It means staying curious, seeking understanding, and remaining invested in your role. When you decide to remain still, opportunities quietly pass by, and time moves forward without progress.

The public deserves employees who care enough to stay sharp. Challenging yourself strengthens not only your own career but the entire service system. Small steps matter. Learning a new process, participating in training, or volunteering for a project keeps your service meaningful and relevant.

Accepting dead-end service is more than a personal loss; it is a disservice to the mission. Each government employee plays a role in maintaining strong, effective public service. Never let comfort become your ceiling. Keep growing, keep learning, and keep moving forward. That is how service remains alive, and how a career becomes something you can stand behind with pride.

24

Fear of Improvements to the Mission

C hange within government is inevitable. Over time, priorities shift, communities evolve, and the needs of the public transform. What worked ten years ago may no longer serve the same purpose today. This is not a sign of failure; it is a natural part of progress. Yet many government employees struggle with mission changes, especially when those changes disrupt familiar routines and established ways of working.

Government missions change for many reasons. Elections bring new leadership, policies evolve with social expectations, budgets shift with economic conditions, and technology advances at an unprecedented pace. Each of these factors influences how agencies operate. When employees resist these changes, agencies risk falling behind and losing connection with the people they are meant to serve.

Accepting mission change does not mean agreeing with every new policy or direction. It means remaining flexible, professional, and willing to learn. When missions evolve, our responsibility as public servants is to adapt and continue delivering quality service under the new vision. Change challenges us to grow, to think differently, and to find better ways to meet public needs.

Resistance to change often stems from fear. Fear of losing control. Fear of not understanding new expectations. Fear of becoming irrelevant. These emotions are understandable, but they must be managed with perspective. A change in mission does not erase your value; it reshapes how your value can be applied. With every shift comes an opportunity to learn, contribute, and improve.

Employees who grow with mission changes build resilience. Those who adapt are often the ones who thrive as organizations move forward. Instead of viewing change as a threat, see it as a test of professionalism and adaptability. Ask questions, seek clarity, and take the time to understand how new directions affect your role. Knowledge builds confidence, and confidence reduces fear.

The public relies on government to adjust when circumstances demand it. Whether change is driven by law, leadership, or necessity, the mission must continue. Embracing this truth aligns you with the core of government service: meeting people where they are and responding to their evolving needs.

A true government professional understands that change is not the enemy of stability; it is the reason stability exists. Without progress, service stalls, and relevance fades. Change is how government remains alive, responsive, and effective. When your agency's mission shifts, pause, remember why you serve, and move forward with purpose. Every change is a new opportunity to make an impact. Mission improvements do not take away your place in service; they invite you to help shape its future.

25

Mismanaging Confidence and Weakness in Your Government Service

Confidence is one of the most important qualities a government employee can have. It allows you to take initiative, guide others, and perform your duties with assurance. But confidence must be balanced with self-awareness. When confidence turns into arrogance, it blocks growth. When awareness of weakness turns into insecurity, it paralyzes progress. Both extremes are threats to effective government service.

Many government employees take pride in mastering their positions, and rightfully so. Experience brings efficiency, reliability, and institutional knowledge. However, no matter how long you've served or how skilled you are, government work is never static. Policies change, technology evolve, and public needs shift. When you assume there is nothing left to learn, you quietly begin to fall behind. Arrogance toward your strengths closes the door to improvement and distances you from collaboration.

At the same time, fear of your weaknesses can be just as damaging. Some employees avoid training, new projects, or leadership opportunities because they fear exposure. They retreat from growth rather than engage it. This mindset convinces people that acknowledging a gap in knowledge is failure, when in reality it is the starting point of progress. Government service does not require perfection. It requires honesty, effort, and willingness to learn.

Strong government employees live in the middle ground. They know what they do well, and they are not threatened by what they do not. They use their strengths to support others, not to dominate them. They use their weaknesses as indicators of where to invest time, training, and development. This balance builds credibility and trust among coworkers and supervisors alike.

Mismanaging confidence can also damage workplace culture. Arrogance creates resistance, silences collaboration, and discourages teamwork. Insecurity does the opposite by removing voices that should be contributing. Both outcomes weaken the mission. Government agencies function best when employees are confident enough to contribute and humble enough to improve.

Every government professional should regularly ask two questions. What am I good at, and how can I use that to serve better? What do I need to improve, and what steps am I taking to do so? The answers to these questions determine whether confidence becomes leadership or stagnation.

The best government employees remain students of their service. They stay teachable, curious, and open to correction. They understand that mastery is not an endpoint but a responsibility to keep growing. Confidence shows ability, but humility shows maturity. When those two exist together, they form the foundation of lasting, effective public service.

Your strengths are not a finish line. Your weaknesses are not a verdict. Together, they are a roadmap. When you manage both with honesty and discipline, you protect your growth, your credibility, and the mission you serve.

26

Failure to Protect Institutional Knowledge

One of the most overlooked threats in government service is the failure to protect institutional knowledge. Many agencies struggle to plan for the loss of experience when employees retire, transfer, promote or leave unexpectedly. Critical knowledge often lives in the minds of a few individuals, with no formal effort made to document processes or train backup staff.

This problem is frequently viewed as a management failure, and in many cases, it is. Some leadership teams do not prioritize succession planning or cross-training. Employees may remain in the same position for years without preparing others to step in. When that knowledge walks out the door, agencies are left scrambling, and service quality suffers.

However, this issue is not solely management's responsibility. As discussed in other threats, there are moments when working-level staff have opportunities to support the mission even when leadership fails to act. Institutional knowledge is one of those opportunities.

Once you have mastered your own position, there is value in learning how adjacent roles function. Gaining insight into key processes beyond your immediate duties prepares you to step in when gaps arise. This not only protects the agency, but also strengthens your own career by expanding your skill set and usefulness.

Learning institutional knowledge allows multiple goals to be achieved at once. It positions you as a reliable resource, increases your value to the organization, and ensures continuity of service for the public. It also creates flexibility during emergencies, staffing shortages, or unexpected transitions.

Many employees avoid learning additional responsibilities because the work is unfamiliar, complex, or simply unappealing. Ironically, these are often the very areas that provide the greatest growth opportunities. Those who are willing to learn what others avoid often find themselves trusted, respected, and well-positioned for advancement.

Protecting institutional knowledge is an act of service. It ensures that government functions do not depend on a single individual and that the mission continues regardless of personnel changes. By choosing to learn beyond your assigned role, you help stabilize the organization while investing in your own professional future.

Government service depends on continuity. When knowledge is preserved, shared, and passed forward, agencies remain resilient. When it is ignored, service weakens. Choosing to protect institutional knowledge is choosing to serve both the mission and the future.

27

Failing to Establish Short- and Long-Term Career Goals

One of the most overlooked threats to a successful government career is failing to establish clear short- and long-term career goals. Many government employees work hard every day but never pause to ask themselves where their career is actually going. Without direction, even the most dedicated service can become reactive rather than intentional.

Government careers rarely unfold by accident. While some opportunities appear unexpectedly, long-term success is most often the result of planning, preparation, and consistency.

Knowing where you are in your career, where you want to go, and how you intend to get there provides structure and purpose to your service. Without goals, it is easy to drift, become stagnant, or feel disconnected from the mission.

Short-term goals serve as immediate guideposts. These goals might include completing a certification, improving performance in a specific area, learning a new system, or gaining experience in a different function within your agency. Short-term goals keep you engaged and focused on measurable progress. They also help you build momentum and confidence as you develop professionally.

Long-term goals define your broader vision. They force you to think beyond your current position and consider where you want to be five, ten, or twenty years into your career. Whether your goal is to promote, become a subject-matter expert, move into leadership, or broaden your impact through specialized service, long-term goals provide direction. They help you identify what experience, education, and exposure you will need to reach that destination.

Without clearly defined goals, it is easy to work hard without moving forward. Many government employees become frustrated not because they lack ability, but because they lack a plan. This often leads to feeling overlooked, undervalued, or stuck. Goal setting creates accountability. It allows you to evaluate your progress honestly and make adjustments when needed.

Government service is constantly evolving. Agencies change, leadership shifts, and missions are redefined. Having established goals allows you to adapt without losing direction. When your environment changes, your goals can change as well, but the act of planning keeps you intentional rather than reactive. Just as organizations adjust strategies to meet new demands, government employees must be willing to revise their goals as opportunities and responsibilities evolve.

Failing to establish short- and long-term career goals does not mean you lack ambition. Often, it simply means no one taught you to think this way. But growth in government service requires ownership of your career. Planning does not guarantee success, but failing to plan almost always guarantees stagnation.

Your government career should not simply happen to you. It should be something you actively build. Establishing clear goals keeps you focused, motivated, and prepared. When opportunity arrives, you are not scrambling to catch up, you are already moving forward with purpose. That is how meaningful careers are shaped, and how effective public servants are made.

28

Misunderstanding the Role of Junior and Tenured Employees in Government Service

Every government agency has a living system. It grows, adapts, and sustains itself through a balance of experience and renewal. Junior employees often enter government service with fresh perspectives, modern training, and new ways of thinking. Tenured employees bring institutional knowledge, historical context, and hard-earned lessons learned through years of service. When either group misunderstands the role of the other, the mission suffers.

A common mistake in government service is assuming that tenure alone equates to relevance or that newness automatically equates to innovation. Junior employees may be viewed as inexperienced or out of touch with "how things really work," while tenured employees may be unfairly labeled as resistant to change. These assumptions create unnecessary divisions that weaken collaboration and stall progress.

Tenured employees play a critical role in maintaining continuity. They understand why certain systems exist, what has failed in the past, and how policy, politics, and public expectations intersect over time. Their responsibility is not only to perform their duties but to transfer knowledge, explain context, and mentor those who will eventually carry the mission forward.

At the same time, junior employees are not simply there to observe and wait their turn. They often identify inefficiencies, outdated practices, or missed opportunities precisely because they are not yet conditioned to accept "this is how we've always done it." When properly guided, their ideas can strengthen service rather than disrupt it. Ignoring or dismissing these contributions out of insecurity or hierarchy wastes valuable potential.

Problems arise when tenured staff feel threatened by new ideas or when junior staff attempt to change systems without first understanding them. True progress requires both learning and listening. Junior employees must take the time to understand the mission, policies, and history of their agency before proposing change. Tenured employees must remain open enough to consider improvements without viewing them as personal criticism.

The strongest government sections are those where experience and innovation work together. Mentorship replaces gatekeeping. Questions are encouraged instead of silenced. Ideas are evaluated based on merit, not tenure. When junior and tenured employees understand their complementary roles, agencies avoid stagnation on one end and chaos on the other.

Misunderstanding these roles leads to high turnover, low morale, and lost institutional knowledge. Understanding them builds continuity, trust, and sustainable improvement. Government service depends on both those who carry its history and those who shape its future. When each respects the role of the other, the mission remains strong, adaptable, and effective.

·

29

Ignoring the Subculture of Your Agency's Workplace Environment

Now that we've discussed the importance of understanding your agency's workplace culture, the next question is simple: how do you contribute to it? Every employee, regardless of title or tenure, plays a role in shaping the environment they work in. The way you communicate, respond to challenges, and treat your coworkers influences the culture around you every day. Whether that influence is positive or negative depends entirely on your choices.

A positive contribution should always be the priority. Every workplace, especially in government benefits when employees bring professionalism, encouragement, and solutions instead of frustration and blame. Negativity spreads quickly, and once it takes hold, it becomes difficult to reverse. When you focus on what strengthens teamwork and service, you help build a culture that supports everyone, including yourself.

Ask yourself what your agency truly needs to improve its mission. Does it need better communication between divisions? More consistency in difficult sections? A fresh perspective on outdated processes? Once you identify those needs, consider how your personal strengths can help meet them. Everyone has something to offer patience, problem-solving, creativity, reliability. These seemingly small acts of professionalism create ripples that influence the entire organization.

One of the most effective ways to positively impact workplace subculture is to take on challenges others avoid. Every government organization has sections, shifts, or responsibilities that are routinely neglected because no one wants them. These areas often struggle not because they are impossible, but because they lack attention and ownership. If you have the skill, patience, or mindset to step into those spaces, do it. Doing so strengthens the agency and signals leadership rooted in service.

Contributing positively does not mean agreeing with everything or ignoring problems. It means addressing challenges constructively, focusing on solutions instead of complaints, and maintaining professionalism even when others do not. Every agency has people who talk about what is wrong. The ones who act to make things better are the ones who create lasting change.

Government service is not just about doing your job it is about improving the system you are part of. The culture of service thrives when employees care enough to make it better. Whether it is supporting a struggling coworker, volunteering for a difficult assignment, or offering a thoughtful idea to improve workflow, your actions matter.

When you bring consistency, professionalism, and initiative to your work environment, you become part of the reason your agency succeeds. The public may never see these daily contributions, but the results will be visible in smoother operations, stronger morale, and better service delivery. The strongest workplace cultures are built by employees who take pride not only in what they do, but in how they help others do it better.

30

Existing in Workplace Mobbing

orkplace mobbing is a form of collective bullying in which a group of employees or management targets an individual through persistent criticism, exclusion, intimidation, or spreading rumors. Unlike isolated workplace conflict, mobbing is systematic and often long term unless it is confronted and stopped. It creates a hostile environment that damages not only the targeted employee, but the integrity and effectiveness of the organization itself.

In government service, workplace mobbing is especially destructive. Public agencies depend on teamwork, transparency, and trust to function properly. When mobbing takes hold, it silences capable employees, drives out talent, and erodes professionalism. The damage does not stop with the individual being targeted. The mission itself begins to suffer. When fear replaces collaboration, service quality declines.

For the employee being targeted, the effects can be severe. Ongoing isolation, humiliation, and unfair treatment create emotional and psychological strain. Many victims experience anxiety, depression, loss of confidence, and physical stress symptoms. Coming to work becomes an act of survival rather than service. What once felt like meaningful public work becomes a daily source of fear and uncertainty. These experiences often follow employees' home, affecting their health, relationships, and sense of self.

There are instances where management is aware that workplace mobbing is occurring and fails to act. Sometimes this inaction is rooted in the belief that the behavior is not serious enough to address. Other times, leadership avoids intervention to escape conflict or accountability. This failure creates space for informal power structures to grow. When employees believe that harmful behavior is tolerated, it spreads. The unspoken message becomes, "If management allows it, why should I stop?" That mindset fuels toxic environments defined by exclusion, gossip, withheld information, and deliberate obstruction of opportunity, none of which relate to performance or productivity.

Over time, mobbing reshapes workplace culture. Employees learn to stay silent to protect themselves. They avoid speaking up, offering ideas, or challenging poor behavior for fear of becoming the next target. Favoritism replaces fairness. Backroom conversations replace transparency. Productivity drops, innovation disappears, and trust erodes. The agency becomes driven by fear instead of purpose, and the public ultimately pays the price.

This environment often leads to formal complaints, union involvement, and increased operational strain. Employees subjected to mobbing may file Equal Employment Opportunity complaints, seek transfers, or disengage emotionally while remaining physically present. Others leave entirely. These actions are rarely impulsive. They are last resorts taken by individuals trying to protect their dignity, health, and careers. Unfortunately, these moments often expose how unprepared some agencies are to address workplace mobbing effectively.

As a result, government agencies lose experienced, capable employees not because of lack of commitment, but because the environment has become intolerable. Institutional knowledge walks out the door. Morale declines. Remaining staff absorb additional workloads while trust in leadership weakens. When agencies lose people this way, it is not simply a staffing issue. It is a mission failure.

An agency is known not only for how it serves the public, but for how it treats its employees. Those reputations do not always align. High turnover, low morale, and declining productivity are symptoms of deeper internal problems. When these patterns exist, the question is not whether there is a cultural issue, but what leadership is doing or failing to do to address it.

Agencies must take deliberate action to prevent workplace mobbing at its core. This requires more than generic policies. It requires proactive leadership, clear reporting channels, consistent accountability, and protection against retaliation. Training must equip both management and staff to recognize mobbing behaviors early and intervene before harm spreads. Leadership that ignores mobbing protects dysfunction, not the mission.

For employees, existing in workplace mobbing should never be normalized. As discussed in Threat 11, Failure to Take Up for Yourself in Workplace Mobbing, silence may feel like safety, but it often allows harm to deepen. Employees who document behavior, seek support, and assert boundaries are not disrupting the workplace. They are protecting it. No one should be expected to endure abuse in the name of service.

Workplace mobbing thrives in secrecy and collapses under accountability. When government employees and leaders confront it together, they restore fairness, trust, and professionalism. Public service cannot thrive in fear. It thrives in environments where employees are treated with dignity, where truth is protected, and where standing up for what is right is recognized as strength, not rebellion.

Government service is not just about completing tasks. It is about protecting the system that allows service to exist at all. A culture of service survives when employees and leaders care enough to challenge what harms it. When dignity is defended and professionalism is upheld, the mission remains strong, resilient, and worthy of the public's trust.

31

Attempting to Dictate the Direction of Government as a Worker

In many ways, we as government staff take ownership of our place in government. We care about the work, the mission, and the people we serve. This sense of ownership can be healthy because it shows pride, accountability, and dedication to the role we play. However, there is a fine line between ownership and possession. When we begin to view our section, our programs, or even our agencies as ours to control, we cross into a mindset that can damage both the service and the mission.

A possessive approach to government service occurs when employees believe they alone define how things should operate, regardless of leadership, policy, or public need. It's an attitude that says, "This is my way, my department, my position," rather than, "This is the public's service, and I am entrusted to help manage it." While it's easy to fall into this mindset after years of experience, it's important to remember that government does not belong to us; it belongs to the people we serve.

In government, change is constant. Politicians are elected, new directors are appointed, and the public continues to evolve in what it expects from its institutions. When we cling too tightly to "how things have always been," we create resistance to progress. This resistance often leads to frustration, especially when the direction of leadership or public demand does not align with our personal views. The result is conflict between employees and management, and between the agency and the mission.

A possessive mindset also limits collaboration. When employees feel territorial over programs, information, or authority, teamwork breaks down. The focus shifts from serving the mission to protecting personal control. This behavior creates barriers between sections and discourages innovation, as new ideas are viewed as threats rather than opportunities.

This threat is closely connected to *Failure to Protect Institutional Knowledge* and *Approaching Government Service as Something You "Own."* While those threats address the preservation of information and identity-level entitlement, this one focuses on behavior. Attempting to dictate the direction of government reflects a shift from contribution to control. When influence is driven by personal authority rather than stewardship, dedication turns into obstruction, and service suffers as a result.

The truth is that no one person owns the work of government. We are all stewards, temporary caretakers of a system designed to serve the public good. Our duty is to maintain it, improve it, and pass it forward in better condition than we found it. That requires humility and flexibility, not rigidity or dominance. Taking pride in your work is a strength. Treating it as personal property is not. Government service is a shared mission that depends on collaboration, communication, and respect for the larger system.

Remember that public service is trust, not territory. Your influence matters, but it must always align with the public interest. When stewardship replaces ownership, we remain adaptable, cooperative, and mission-driven, regardless of who leads or what changes come. Government may employ us, but it belongs to the people. Our responsibility is not to control it, but to serve it with integrity, professionalism, and respect for its constant evolution.

32

Fear of Government Turnover

Government turnover is inevitable. It is part of the natural rhythm of public service. Directors retire, elected officials change, policies shift, and employees move on to new roles or agencies. Some government entities experience this slowly over decades, while others face constant transitions. Either way, change is unavoidable, and how we respond to it defines our professionalism and adaptability.

Over time, government employees can grow comfortable. Familiar missions, stable leadership, and consistent coworkers create a sense of predictability. When that stability is disrupted by turnover, anxiety and uncertainty often follow. Questions arise about new leadership, shifting priorities, and personal job security. These concerns are natural, but they should not dictate how we perform or how we view our role in service.

As discussed in earlier threats such as *Being Fearful of Management and Your Administration* and *Accepting Stagnancy Within Your Service*, comfort can be misleading. It creates the illusion of permanence in a system designed to evolve. Government turnover is not inherently negative. In many cases, it brings renewal. New leadership can introduce fresh perspectives, updated practices, and renewed energy, especially in agencies where stagnation has taken hold.

Fear of turnover is usually rooted in uncertainty rather than the change itself. Employees may worry about losing influence, being misunderstood, or being asked to adapt to unfamiliar expectations. But adaptability is one of the most valuable skills in government service. Turnover tests not only technical ability, but also emotional intelligence, resilience, and professionalism.

Instead of fearing turnover, it should be viewed as an opportunity to learn, refocus, and grow. Each leadership transition brings lessons. Each staffing change invites reflection on your role, your skills, and your readiness for what comes next. Public needs evolve over time, and the people who serve them must evolve as well. The strongest government employees maintain mission focus regardless of who is in charge.

Turnover can also open doors. A department long anchored in tradition may benefit from leadership willing to challenge outdated processes. A supervisor's departure may create opportunities for growth, advancement, or expanded responsibility. Even difficult transitions often produce long-term benefits for individuals and agencies alike.

Fear thrives in uncertainty, but preparation builds confidence. When you invest in your development, remain informed, and stay flexible, turnover becomes part of your career journey rather than a threat to it. Government service is not about permanence. It is about progress.

The best government employees accept that change is part of the mission itself. Leaders will come and go, but the work continues. The uniform, the badge, the desk, or the role may look the same, but the people behind them will change over time. When you accept this truth, fear loses its grip. Turnover may change faces, but it should never change your commitment to serve.

33

Lack of Interagency Collaboration or Cooperation

Interagency cohesiveness works much like a roof truss system. Each beam supports the others, distributing weight evenly to hold the entire structure in place. When one beam fails, the system weakens. When all parts connect and work together, the structure stands strong. This is how effective interagency collaboration should function in government. Each section, division, or department carries its share of the mission while supporting others to maintain stability and effectiveness.

Every government agency is built on cooperation. Administration, operations, finance, logistics, enforcement, and support services all play different roles, but they share a common goal: effective service to the public. When collaboration is strong, communication flows more freely, problems are resolved faster, and outcomes improve. When agencies or internal sections compete, isolate themselves, or withhold information, the system weakens. The result is inefficiency, declining morale, and frustration for the public.

A lack of interagency collaboration often stems from personal bias, territorial thinking, or poor communication between leadership and staff. In some cases, employees treat authority, resources, or access as leverage rather than shared responsibility. This behavior may feel like protecting one's section, but it ultimately undermines professionalism and delays progress. When one group refuses to cooperate, everyone pays the price, especially the public.

Strong agencies understand that no single division can complete the mission alone. Collaboration means acknowledging interdependence. Your success depends on others doing their part just as theirs depends on you. When this mindset is embraced, barriers dissolve and teamwork replace rivalry. The focus shifts from credit and control to outcomes and service.

This threat connects directly to earlier discussions such as Misunderstanding the Role of Junior and Tenured Employees in Government Service *and* Attempting to Dictate the Direction of Government as a Worker. Both highlight how ego, territorial behavior, and resistance to collaboration quietly erode effectiveness. True cooperation requires humility, the willingness to share information, accept support, and recognize the value others bring.

When collaboration breaks down, the damage spreads quickly. Projects stall, communication fractures, and resentment grows between sections. Over time, these internal failures reach the public in the form of delayed services, conflicting information, or poor outcomes. The cost of disunity is paid in time, resources, and trust.

When agencies and divisions work together, the opposite occurs. Morale improves, innovation increases, and service delivery becomes more efficient. Collaboration strengthens not only outcomes, but also credibility. The public experiences a government that operates as a unified system rather than disconnected parts.

Government service is not a solo effort. It is a coordinated structure that relies on every part doing its job while supporting others in doing theirs. A culture of cooperation ensures that the system remains balanced, resilient, and capable of carrying the weight of public trust. When government works together, the mission does not just succeed, it rises.

34

Being Emotionally Dependent on Recognition

Recognition from leadership feels good, and it should. A sincere compliment, a public acknowledgment, or even a quiet "thank you" can affirm that our work matters. When recognition is fair and genuine, it can motivate and reinforce purpose. However, there is a critical difference between appreciating recognition and becoming emotionally dependent on it. When self-worth or work ethic begins to rely on praise, the foundation of service shifts away from the mission and toward validation.

Government employees often work in high-pressure environments where recognition is inconsistent or rare. Some leaders actively acknowledge good work, while others focus only on deficiencies or results. If your motivation rises and falls based on whether leadership notices you, disappointment can begin to shape your performance. Public service demands consistency. The public deserves your best effort whether recognition comes or not, because service is built on responsibility, not applause.

As discussed in Practicing Emotional Intelligence with the Ups and Downs of Your Service, emotional discipline is essential. Dependence on recognition creates instability. Motivation spikes when praise is given and drops when it is absent. This emotional fluctuation distracts from the mission and places your sense of value in someone else's control. The most professional government employees learn to self-validate through integrity, results, and adherence to standards, even when no one is watching.

Leadership does carry responsibility for recognizing effort fairly and consistently. When that does not happen, frustration is understandable. Still, maturity in government service requires channeling that frustration into discipline rather than disengagement. Measuring success by impact instead of attention builds resilience. Quiet achievers, those who complete difficult tasks, support others, and uphold standards without recognition, are often the true backbone of an agency.

Emotional independence from recognition does not mean indifference. Appreciation still matters and should be valued when it comes. The difference is that your commitment does not depend on it. Professionalism means showing up with the same effort whether recognition follows or not. Integrity does not fluctuate with praise.

Recognition fades. Titles change. Leadership turns over. What remains is your reputation, your work ethic, and the impact you leave behind. When you serve faithfully and consistently, you build something more durable than applause. Let your work speak for itself. In government service, real recognition is found not in what is said about you, but in what continues to work because you did your job well.

35

Allowing Conflict and Shortcomings to Influence Your Commitment

As noted throughout this book, a government career will always include periods of progress and periods of difficulty. These moments test more than patience; they test professionalism. When leadership is supportive, teamwork is strong, and operations run smoothly, commitment comes easily. Pride in the mission feels natural. But when conflict emerges, communication breaks down, or leadership fails to lead, discouragement can set in. The real danger begins when those moments are allowed to dictate commitment to the service itself.

It is easy to remain motivated when the environment feels fair and supportive. It is far more difficult when you feel overlooked, unheard, or frustrated by systemic shortcomings. Over time, some government employees drift into what can be described as a "retirement mindset," showing up only to endure rather than to contribute. This gradual disengagement does not happen all at once. It happens quietly, and it harms not only the individual, but the mission, the team, and ultimately the public.

Conflict in government service is inevitable. New leaders bring different approaches, policies evolve, and coworkers come and go. Challenges will arise that test resolve and patience. What defines professionalism is not the absence of conflict, but the response to it. Allowing frustration, disappointment, or institutional failure to weaken effort or attitude undermines the very purpose of public service. Government does not exist to meet personal comfort. It exists to serve the public consistently, even when conditions are imperfect.

True commitment is not dependent on who is in charge or how others perform. It is internal. It is the decision to continue doing the right thing regardless of recognition, morale, or circumstance. It is choosing professionalism over resentment, discipline over disengagement, and purpose over frustration. Every task completed with integrity contributes to the mission, even when appreciation feels distant or absent.

As discussed in earlier threats such as Practicing Emotional Intelligence with the Ups and Downs of Your Service *and* Fear of Government Turnover, the strongest employees remain steady amid disruption. They adapt without losing focus. They acknowledge challenges without allowing them to define their attitude. They step back, when necessary, recover, and return grounded in purpose.

Government service is a long journey. Some days will test resolve more than others. Through those moments, commitment must be anchored in something greater than circumstance. The public does not see internal politics, leadership failures, or workplace conflict. They see outcomes. Remaining committed to quality service, regardless of internal shortcomings, ensures the public receives what it deserves.

Stay steady. Stay professional. Let consistency speak louder than conflict. While frustration and imperfection will come and go, commitment is what defines a true public servant.

36

Ignoring all signs that it is time to move forward in your career

This threat is one that requires honest self-reflection. Every government employee has a unique experience, shaped by the work they do, the people they serve, and the environment they operate in. Over time, we settle into our roles. The work becomes familiar. We understand expectations, routines, and likely outcomes. That familiarity can feel like security. Day after day, we generally know what tomorrow will look like. For some, that predictability is enough. For others, it quietly becomes a signal.

Many government employees feel motivated and committed to service, yet sense internally that it may be time to move forward. That movement can take many forms: promotion, transfer, or even transitioning to a different agency altogether. While not everyone knows exactly where they should go next, many know when something has changed. That internal awareness is often the first sign.

Too often, those signs are ignored. Some employees remain in positions that no longer challenge them or provide opportunities for growth. Others stay in roles where opportunities exist but personal motivation has diminished. A government career can span twenty, twenty-five, or even thirty years. Some employees thrive by staying in one section for an entire career. There is nothing wrong with that. The issue arises when staying is driven by fear, comfort, or habit rather than purpose.

This threat is closely related to Staying Too Comfortable Within Your Position, which highlights the importance of continued challenges. But there is an important distinction. There may come a point where you truly have done all you can do in a role. You have improved systems, strengthened operations, and explored every reasonable avenue for growth. At that point, continuing to "push harder" may no longer serve the mission or you.

This threat is not about coasting or simply surviving the workday. It applies to employees who have given genuine effort, invested in improvement, and taken their role seriously. Sometimes, loving the mission does not mean staying in the same place forever. It means continuing that service in a different capacity.

As discussed in Fear of Transferring Service Positions, many government employees hesitate to move because of uncertainty. Transfers can feel like starting over. New systems, new expectations, and new relationships create discomfort. Yet over time, experience across multiple sections often produces a broader, more adaptable skill set. For many employees, transferring every five to seven years builds depth, perspective, and long-term value. This approach is not for everyone, but for some, it aligns naturally with their drive to grow.

The decision to move forward should never be impulsive. Strong managers may not want to lose effective employees and may even discourage movement. That resistance is not always negative; it often reflects appreciation. But before deciding whether to stay or go, honest questions must be asked. Have I done all I can in this role? Am I seeking to expand my service, or am I avoiding something difficult? Am I leaving to grow, or leaving to escape?

There is also something humbling about leaving a position you are good at to step into one where you must learn again. That uncertainty is what keeps many employees rooted in place long after their growth has slowed. Consider an employee managing vehicles for a government inspection office. Over several years, they improve tracking, purchasing, and replacement processes. Operations run smoothly. Supervisors are satisfied. Inspectors are supported. The mission is being met. Eventually, improvements plateau. Effort turns into maintenance rather than progress. Meanwhile, other vacant positions within the agency stand out as places where new impact could be made.

Ignoring that pull often leads to gradual disengagement. Motivation fades. Initiative declines. The work remains functional, but no longer energizing. Staying for the "long haul" begins to feel less like commitment and more like endurance. Government will continue its mission regardless of who fills which position. While individual talent matters, no role exists solely because of one person. Wanting to feel needed is natural, but growth rarely comes from repeating the same effort with diminishing enthusiasm. When initiative fades, value fades with it.

This threat comes down to a simple truth: most government employees recognize the moment when it is time to move forward. Ignoring that awareness does not preserve stability; it delays growth. Moving forward does not mean abandoning service. It means choosing to apply your experience where it can grow again.

Sometimes, the most meaningful progress in a government career does not come from working harder where you are, but from having the courage to continue the journey somewhere new.

37

Seeking Legacy Over Service

Many members of the public recognize famous political figures or appointed officials whose legacies are celebrated openly. Within the inner workings of government, however, there are also quiet legends. These are individuals whose influence lives on through procedures they built, programs they shaped, or people they mentored long after they retired. The key question is this: did they set out to be remembered, or did their legacy emerge naturally from how they served?

It is natural for government employees to want their work to matter beyond their years of service. Many dedicate decades of their lives to public work, and it is human to hope that those efforts leave a mark. The problem arises when the desire to be remembered becomes more important than the responsibility to serve. Seeking a legacy is not the same as building one. When recognition of future impact overshadows present duty, priorities quietly shift away from the mission.

This threat is distinct from others that focus on attention or praise. Fame and Glory Seeking address the pursuit of recognition during one's career. Legacy seeking is more subtle. It often disguises itself as vision, ambition, or passion. When employees begin to focus on how history will remember them, humility can erode. Decisions become influenced by perception rather than necessity, and by personal imprint rather than public outcome.

This mindset can shape behavior in damaging ways. A manager may favor projects that carry their name instead of those that best serve the community. An employee may resist changes that improve service because they threaten a system they personally built. Over time, legacy-driven thinking can foster ego, favoritism, and resistance to progress. The mission becomes secondary to preservation of an image.

In reality, the most meaningful legacies in government are rarely intentional. They are created by those who focused on doing the work well, every day, without concern for how it would be remembered. These individuals trained others to succeed, shared knowledge freely, and strengthened systems without needing credit. Their influence endured because it was embedded in the service itself, not attached to their identity.

Legacy is not found in plaques, awards, or stories repeated in hallways. It is found in continuity. It lives in the people who carry the work forward, the systems that function better because you were there, and the problems that no longer exist because you helped solve them. Names fade. Processes remain. Communities continue.

The irony of legacy in government is this: the more you chase it, the less likely it is to last. But when you focus fully on serving the mission in front of you, your impact has a way of surviving on its own. Let service be your priority and allow legacy, if it comes at all, to be a byproduct rather than the goal.

38

Approaching Government Service as Something You "Own"

Many of us who work in government develop a deep connection to our agencies. We dedicate years of effort, pride, and care to the mission, and through that commitment, a sense of ownership naturally forms. We say things like "my office," "my department," or "my vehicle," not out of arrogance, but because of personal investment. However, there is a critical difference between taking ownership of our effort and believing we own government itself.

Government service belongs to the people, not to those who provide it. The buildings, vehicles, authority, and resources we use exist to serve the public, not to establish personal territory. While the public does not directly step into our roles, the authority we hold is not ours by right. It is entrusted to us by the citizens we serve. Our responsibility is not to claim that authority, but to manage it with humility, transparency, and accountability.

The danger arises when this distinction is lost. When government employees begin operating as if their agency belongs to them, the mission quietly shifts. "Government for the people" becomes "government for ourselves." This mindset breeds entitlement, power struggles, and resistance to oversight. Instead of ensuring access, fairness, and equity, we form barriers between employees and the public. This also includes barriers between purpose and practice.

This threat connects directly to several other themes in this book. In Personal Agenda vs. Service Tasks, we examined how personal motives can interfere with the mission. In Seeking Legacy Over Service, we explored how self-focus can overshadow public responsibility. In Mismanaging Confidence and Weakness in Your Government Service, we saw how pride can distort judgment. Approaching government service as something you "own" is the point where these threats converge into a fundamental misunderstanding of role and responsibility.

Taking ownership of your work ethic is essential. Taking pride in your contribution is healthy. Taking responsibility for outcomes is professional. But taking possession of government itself its direction, its authority, or its resources is misguided.

Government is a living system built on law, policy, and public trust. It serves everyone, including those we agree with and those we do not. When personal control replaces stewardship, the spirit of service erodes.

True professionalism in government is not about dominance or permanence. It is about stewardship. It means caring for public resources as if they matter deeply, while never forgetting they are not ours to claim. It means safeguarding trust, ensuring fairness, and recognizing that we are temporary caretakers in a system designed to outlast us.

The greatest pride in government service does not come from control, but from contribution. When you leave a position stronger than you found it, when systems function better because of your effort, and when access improves because of your decisions, you have done your part. Government does not belong to us, but our integrity, discipline, and professionalism absolutely do.

So, when you say, "my office" or "my department," let it mean something intentional. Let it mean the place where you give your best, not the place you claim yours. Because when we remember who government truly belongs to, service remains grounded, power remains accountable, and trust remains intact.

39

Inability to Help Others with Their Government Service

Who needs help in government? We often think first of the public as the primary recipient of government service. But what about the people who make that service possible? Government employees need help too. From the worker struggling to keep up with new demands to the new hire still learning systems and expectations, internal support is just as essential as the services delivered to the public.

Yes, agencies offer formal resources such as Employee Assistance Programs, training initiatives, and wellness services.

Those systems matter. But just as important is the daily, informal support that occurs between coworkers. A few encouraging words, shared experience, practical guidance, or a willingness to collaborate can make the difference between someone surviving their role and succeeding in it. As discussed in Judging Coworkers with Different Work Ethics Than You, we all approach work differently. Helping others succeed, even when their pace, style, or methods differ from our own, strengthens the entire team.

Many government employees work in sections that support other government functions rather than interacting directly with the public. This is the unseen backbone of public service government that supports government. Whether you work in logistics, information technology, finance, human resources, or administration, your role likely enables others to serve the public effectively. And just as those employees depend on your work, you depend on theirs. When cooperation exists at every level, the system holds together. When it does not, breakdowns ripple outward, as described in Lack of Interagency Collaboration or Cooperation.

The threat emerges when help is intentionally withheld. Fear, insecurity, jealousy, resentment, or personal bias can cause employees to step back when they should step forward. This behavior often connects directly to Personal Agenda vs. Service Tasks, where individual motives interfere with the mission. When we withhold assistance because we fear someone else's success might diminish our own standing, we shift the focus away from service and toward self-preservation.

Helping others does not require authority, title, or formal responsibility. It requires humility and awareness. It requires recognizing that your effectiveness is linked to the effectiveness of those around you. As discussed in Not Taking Ownership of Your Government Service, ownership includes responsibility beyond your own tasks. Supporting coworkers is part of that responsibility because their success contributes directly to the mission's success.

When employees refuse to help one another, morale drops, silos form, and performance weakens. Knowledge stays trapped, errors multiply, and frustration grows. When help is extended freely, collaboration improves, confidence increases, and productivity stabilizes. Small actions guiding a coworker through a process, sharing lessons learned, offering ideas to improve workflow, or simply being available can change the tone of an entire section or agency.

The inability to help others is not just a personal limitation; it is a service breakdown. As explored in Allowing Conflict and Shortcomings to Influence Your Commitment, challenges are inevitable. But when employees support one another through those challenges, resilience increases. Government service is not a competition for visibility or advancement. It is a shared responsibility built on collective capability.

Helping others does not diminish your value; it multiplies it. Teaching what you know strengthens the system. Supporting those still learning ensures continuity. When government employees invest in one another, the mission becomes stronger than any single role or individual. In the end, the capacity of government is not measured by isolated excellence, but by how well its people help one another carry the work forward.

40

Getting Others to Do Your Service Work for You

What does it mean to work hard in government? What does it mean to fall short of that standard? Ask ten people, and you may get ten different answers. Some define hard work as going beyond expectations. Others define it as doing exactly what is required with consistency and accuracy. But regardless of perspective, one principle remains non-negotiable: you are responsible for your assigned work. Government service operates on accountability, and when that accountability erodes, the mission weakens.

In every agency, there are employees who carry their share of responsibility. They show up prepared, take ownership of their duties, and follow through without being chased. There are also employees who quietly shift their responsibilities onto others. They blur the line between collaboration and avoidance, disguise manipulation as teamwork, and frame inaction as efficiency. This behavior is not harmless. It damages morale, erodes trust, and places an unfair burden on those who continue to do their work with integrity.

As discussed in Not Taking Ownership of Your Government Service, accountability begins with understanding that your duties belong to you. Collaboration is expected in government work, but collaboration does not mean transferring responsibility. Persuading or relying on coworkers to complete your assigned tasks under the pretense of "helping out" is not delegation. It is avoidance. Over time, this behavior becomes predatory, exploiting the reliability of others while contributing less to the mission.

Some justify this conduct by claiming they are "too busy" or focused on "higher-level priorities." Others take advantage of coworkers who are naturally helpful or reluctant to say no. These patterns often appear subtly: unfinished reports quietly completed by teammates, deadlines repeatedly rescued by others, or responsibilities informally reassigned without acknowledgment. Each instance may seem minor, but together they create imbalance, resentment, and fatigue across a team.

This threat also connects to Allowing Conflict and Shortcomings to Influence Your Commitment. When motivation declines or frustration grows, some employees disengage rather than address the issue directly. Instead of seeking support, adjusting workload, or having honest conversations with supervisors, they shift their responsibilities onto others. While the causes may vary, burnout, resentment, complacency, the outcome is consistent: someone else absorbs work that was never theirs to carry.

Healthy teamwork, as explored in Inability to Help Others with Their Government Service, depends on reciprocity and trust. Helping a coworker is not the same as being used by one. Support must flow in both directions. When one person consistently avoids responsibility, it drains the goodwill of others and weakens the collective effort. Over time, strong performers become frustrated, disengaged, or resentful, not because the work is hard, but because the burden is unfair.

In government service, integrity is demonstrated not only through effort, but through ownership. The public expects each employee to contribute honestly to the role they hold. When responsibility is shifted instead of met, accountability breaks down and professionalism suffers.

Before asking someone else to step in, ask yourself why. Is this true collaboration, or avoidance? Is the request balanced, or habitual? Government service depends on shared effort, but shared effort only works when everyone carries their portion. When each employee takes responsibility for their work, teamwork strengthens, trust stabilizes, and the mission moves forward without leaving anyone behind.

41

Traditions Over the Mission

Tradition runs deep in government service. For many agencies, long-standing practices become part of institutional identity. Traditions can provide stability, continuity, and pride. They remind us of how departments were built and of the people who laid the foundation for today's work. When healthy, tradition preserves culture and reinforces a shared sense of purpose.

However, there is a critical difference between honoring tradition and being constrained by it. When tradition becomes so entrenched that it prevents growth, innovation, or modernization, it stops serving the public and starts serving itself. As discussed in

Fear of Improvements to the Mission, government service must evolve alongside the needs of the people. Public expectations change, and the systems designed to meet them must change as well.

Agencies that cling to outdated practices simply because "this is how we've always done it" risk becoming disconnected from the communities they serve. This is not loyalty to tradition it is resistance to progress. Tradition should strengthen the mission, not override it. When procedure is valued more than outcome, service quality declines and relevance erodes.

New employees often bring fresh perspectives that challenge existing methods. Their ideas can reveal inefficiencies, outdated processes, or missed opportunities. Yet when leadership or senior staff dismiss these ideas solely in the name of tradition, agencies lose valuable chances to improve. This resistance closely mirrors the mindset described in Staying Too Comfortable Within Your Position, where familiarity becomes a shield against necessary change.

Tradition can also interfere with collaboration. As explored in Lack of Interagency Collaboration or Cooperation, departments sometimes cling to their own established ways of operating even when cooperation would better serve the mission. When tradition becomes territorial, it isolates rather than unites. The focus shifts from serving the public to protecting a method, reputation, or internal identity.

This threat is not an argument against tradition itself. Strong traditions preserve values like integrity, accountability, and public trust. They provide continuity during times of change. But tradition must remain connected to purpose. When practice no longer supports effective service, it should be reexamined. Government exists to serve current and future needs, not to preserve outdated systems for their own sake.

As communities evolve, so must the institutions that serve them. The question is not whether a tradition is familiar, but whether it still helps the agency fulfill its mission. When tradition blocks improvement, it becomes an obstacle rather than an asset.

The strongest agencies strike a balance. They honor their roots while remaining willing to adapt. They treat tradition as a foundation, not a boundary. When the mission leads and tradition follows, government remains relevant, effective, and responsive. Tradition should guide service, not confine it.

42

Giving Up When Management Says No

Government service provides countless opportunities to contribute ideas, develop improvements, and influence meaningful change. Many employees find purpose in proposing new programs, refining processes, or offering suggestions that could strengthen the mission. When those ideas are approved, the result is motivating and affirming. But an equally important question remains: what happens when management says no?

Rejection can be discouraging, especially when an idea feels personal or when significant time and effort have been invested. It is easy to interpret a denial as a lack of appreciation or support.

However, as discussed in Practicing Emotional Intelligence with the Ups and Downs of Your Service, how you respond to disappointment matters just as much as the idea itself. Professional growth does not come from agreement alone. It comes from how we handle resistance.

In many cases, a decision has little to do with the quality of the idea. Budget limitations, policy restrictions, political timing, or broader operational priorities often shape management decisions. A denial may simply reflect circumstances rather than rejection of the concept. When employees allow disappointment to turn into disengagement, the mission suffers. The public still needs consistent service, regardless of internal outcomes.

This moment of rejection connects closely with Allowing Conflict and Shortcomings to Influence Your Commitment. Commitment cannot rise and fall based on approval. True professionalism is revealed when effort remains steady, even after hearing no. Giving up after rejection shifts focus from service to emotion, and over time, that mindset erodes effectiveness and credibility.

Instead of withdrawing, treat rejection as a moment for assessment. Ask constructive questions. Was the proposal clearly communicated? Was additional information needed? Was the timing appropriate? These reflections turn rejection into insight. As emphasized in Not Taking Ownership of Your Government Service, ownership includes responsibility for how you respond when leadership disagrees with you.

There will also be times when management resists change or lacks the willingness to explore new approaches. Even then, giving up rarely produces results. Refining an idea, gathering data, and waiting for the right moment demonstrates maturity and strategic thinking. Government often moves slowly, but persistence supported by preparation is far more effective than frustration or defiance.

Progress in public service requires patience. Improvement is rarely immediate, and influence is often built over time. When employees remain engaged after hearing no, they demonstrate reliability and long-term commitment. These are the individuals who leadership eventually trusts when circumstances change.

Hearing no is not the end of contribution. It is part of learning how your agency works and how to navigate it effectively. When you remain thoughtful, composed, and focused on service rather than outcome, you position yourself for future impact. Not every idea will be accepted, but every response shapes your professional reputation. Stay engaged, stay adaptable, and remember that persistence grounded in professionalism often speaks louder than approval ever could.

43

The Inability to Draw the Line Between Eagerness for Service and Personal Needs

G overnment service naturally attracts people who want to do good. Many of us enter public service with a strong desire to contribute, help others, and make a meaningful difference. That eagerness is honorable and it is often the foundation of high-quality service. However, even the most committed government employee must learn to draw a clear line between dedication to service and the personal needs that every individual carries. When these two areas blur, they create emotional strain, poor boundaries, and professional imbalance.

Throughout this book, several threats touch this issue indirectly. Practicing Emotional Intelligence with the Ups and Downs of Your Service emphasizes managing emotions without allowing them to control decisions. Allowing Conflict and Shortcomings to Influence Your Commitment highlights how stress and frustration can erode purpose. This threat builds on those ideas by addressing a deeper challenge: understanding that government service cannot replace personal fulfillment, emotional validation, or self-worth.

Problems arise when eagerness for service turns into personal dependency. Some employees unconsciously seek approval, belonging, or identity through their work. Others take on excessive responsibility, believing that constant availability proves value or commitment. This pattern closely connects with Fame and Glory Seeking and Seeking Legacy Over Service, where motivation becomes tied to personal identity rather than professional duty.

Unchecked eagerness often stems from unmet needs outside the workplace. For some, service provides pride or purpose they struggle to find elsewhere. For others, work becomes an escape from personal challenges. In these situations, service begins to resemble self-sacrifice instead of professionalism. When that happens, judgment weakens, boundaries fade, and decision-making becomes emotionally driven rather than mission-focused.

When personal needs and service become intertwined, saying no becomes difficult. Employees may overextend themselves, avoid delegation, or feel responsible for fixing everything around them. This mirrors the pattern discussed in When Being Helpful Crosses into Being Used. Without clear boundaries, eagerness shifts from an asset to a liability, affecting not only the individual but the entire workplace.

The reality is this: commitment does not require depletion. You can care deeply without losing yourself in the work. You can give consistently without tying your value to how much you sacrifice. The most effective public servants understand that service is strongest when it is grounded in balance, not emotional dependency.

Drawing that line requires self-awareness and honesty. It means recognizing when motivation is driven by purpose versus personal need. It means asking difficult questions before saying yes. Is this action advancing the mission, or am I seeking validation? Am I serving the public interest, or avoiding something in my personal life?

When that distinction becomes clear, service regains its strength. Decisions become steadier. Boundaries become healthier. Eagerness returns to its proper place as a source of energy rather than exhaustion.

Government service is meant to be sustainable. The public benefits most from employees who are engaged, balanced, and clear-headed. Protecting your personal well-being is not a failure of dedication; it is a requirement for lasting service. When you learn to draw the line, you ensure that your commitment remains strong, your judgment remains sound, and your service remains something you can carry forward with clarity and purpose.

44

Taking Outside Opinions About Your Government Service Personally

O ne of the most surprising experiences for many government employees is discovering how many people believe they understand your job better than you do. This can come from the general public, private-sector workers, media portrayals, and even other government employees who have never performed your specific role. Movies and television dramatize government work. Social media amplifies only extremes. Over time, these portrayals shape opinions that feel confident but are often detached from reality.

This does not only happen outside your agency. Within government itself, adjacent sections or coworkers may speak on what they think your job entails, how easy they believe it is, or how they assume it should be done. Sometimes these comments are inaccurate. Sometimes they minimize the complexity, responsibility, or pressure your position carries. Sometimes they simply overlook how your work supports the broader mission.

Hearing your service misrepresented can be frustrating and even insulting, especially for employees who take pride in their work. That pride is not the problem. The danger appears when outside opinions begin to affect your emotional state, your motivation, or your sense of professional identity. As discussed in Practicing Emotional Intelligence with the Ups and Downs of Your Service, emotional regulation is essential in government work. When uninformed opinions are taken personally, they create resentment, distraction, and unnecessary emotional weight that follows you into the workplace.

The truth is that most people speak from perception, not experience. Their opinions are shaped by headlines, assumptions, or partial information. They rarely see the preparation, responsibility, accountability, and behind-the-scenes effort that government service requires. Their commentary often reflects limited understanding, not the reality of your work. Taking those opinions personally gives them influence they do not deserve.

This threat also connects to Allowing Conflict and Shortcomings to Influence Your Commitment. *When* external criticism seeps into your mindset, your focus shifts from service to defense. Instead of centering on outcomes and responsibility, emotional energy gets spent reacting to misunderstanding. That shift may feel justified, but it pulls attention away from the mission and weakens professional clarity.

In some cases, this sensitivity ties back to Being Emotionally Dependent on Recognition *and* Fame and Glory Seeking. When validation becomes important, criticism naturally feels heavier. Outside opinions gain power when self-worth is attached to how others perceive your service. This is why separating personal identity from public opinion is critical. Your value as a government employee is defined by performance, integrity, and consistency, not by commentary from those outside your role.

This threat also aligns with Approaching Government Service as Something You Own. When service becomes personal territory, outside opinions feel threatening rather than irrelevant. But government service belongs to the people, including those who misunderstand it. Our responsibility is not to convince everyone of our value, but to deliver steady, professional service regardless of perception.

When outside opinions are taken personally, they affect more than emotions. They influence focus, relationships, and decision-making. Over time, frustration replaces purpose, and defensiveness replaces clarity. When that happens, the mission becomes secondary, and the public ultimately absorbs the cost.

The solution is not to ignore feedback entirely, but to evaluate it wisely. Not all opinions deserve emotional investment. Constructive insight from informed sources can strengthen your service. Uninformed criticism does not. Learn to distinguish between the two.

Stand grounded in your role. Let misunderstandings pass without internalizing it. Keep your attention on the people who rely on your work, not those who speculate about it. When you separate outside perception from internal purpose, your professionalism stabilizes and your service remains steady. Your identity in government is not shaped by outside voices. It is shaped by the effort, discipline, and integrity you bring to the mission every day.

45

Staying Put to Avoid Becoming "New Again"

O ne of the quietest fears in government service is not fear of change itself, but fear of becoming "new" again. After years in a position, many employees reach a level of mastery. They know the systems, the people, the shortcuts, and the unspoken rules. Their confidence is earned. Their reputation is established. Over time, that familiarity becomes part of their professional identity. The threat emerges when protecting that identity becomes the reason they refuse to move forward.

Staying in one position can feel safe, not because the work is fulfilling, but because competence has already been proven. Transferring to a new section means starting over in ways that are uncomfortable. It means asking questions again. It means being unfamiliar with processes others take for granted. It means temporarily losing influence, status, and confidence. For many government employees, that temporary discomfort feels like a personal risk they would rather avoid.

This fear is not about laziness or lack of ambition. In many cases, it affects high performers the most. These are employees who are respected, relied upon, and known for getting things done. The idea of entering a new environment where they are no longer the expert can feel like a step backward, even when it is actually a step forward. The longer someone remains in one role, the harder it becomes to imagine being anything other than who they are in that space.

Over time, this avoidance limits growth. Skills become narrow instead of transferable. Perspective becomes fixed instead of expansive. Employees may remain effective in their current role, but disconnected from the broader mission of the agency. When opportunities arise, they are dismissed not because the employee is unqualified, but because the emotional cost of being new again feels too high.

Government service, however, is not designed to reward comfort alone. It is designed to benefit from adaptable, well-rounded professionals who understand the mission from multiple angles. Becoming new again is not a failure of experience. It is proof that experience is being expanded. Every transfer adds depth, context, and resilience to a government career. The temporary discomfort of learning something new strengthens long term effectiveness.

Refusing to move solely to protect familiarity can quietly turn confidence into limitation. The employee may remain reliable but no longer challenged. Over time, motivation fades and curiosity dulls. What once felt like security becomes a ceiling that restricts growth. The fear of being new becomes the very thing that keeps a career from evolving.

Choosing to move does not erase past expertise. It builds on it. Every new role brings opportunities to apply old skills in new ways; to see how different parts of government connect, and to serve the public with a broader understanding of how systems truly work. Growth does not require abandoning who you are. It requires allowing yourself to become more than you are now.

Staying put may feel safe, but growth often begins at the edge of discomfort. Becoming new again is not a loss of identity. It is an investment in your future service. When you are willing to learn again, adapt again, and stretch again, your career remains alive. And when your career continues to grow, so does your ability to serve with depth, perspective, and purpose.

46

Transferring to New Positions Prior to Learning the Old One

Government agencies offer a wide range of opportunities, and with those opportunities comes movement. For some employees, movement becomes the goal itself. They look ahead to the next position before fully understanding the one they currently hold. While ambition has value in government service, moving too quickly can weaken both individual development and the mission as a whole.

This threat is not about fear of change. It is about impatience with growth. In contrast to Staying Put to Avoid Becoming "New"

Again, where employees avoid movement to protect comfort, this threat describes employees who move before they are ready. They leave not because they have mastered their role, but because they are restless, dissatisfied, or eager for something different. In doing so, they carry unfinished learning with them.

Every government position requires time. Some roles can be learned in months. Others take years to fully understand. Beyond tasks, there are systems, relationships, history, and context that shape how the work truly functions. When employees transfer before learning these elements, they lose the opportunity to develop depth. Over time, this creates a career built on surface knowledge rather than real competence.

Ambition without foundation is fragile. In Failing to Establish Short- and Long-Term Career Goals, the importance of intentional planning was emphasized. Purposeful movement requires readiness, not just interest. Transferring simply because a position looks appealing or because the current role feels uncomfortable often results in repeating the same learning gaps in new places. Instead of growth, the employee experiences constant adjustment without mastery.

This pattern affects more than the individual. When employees leave roles prematurely, the remaining team absorbs the cost. Coworkers must cover gaps, correct mistakes, or train replacements without the benefit of proper transition. Over time, this strains morale and weakens continuity. Government service depends on stability built through understanding, not constant turnover driven by impatience.

There is also a long-term consequence that often goes unnoticed. Employees who move too quickly may eventually reach leadership positions without the operational insight needed to lead effectively. They know job titles, but not the work beneath them. This creates blind spots that affect decision-making, credibility, and trust. Government needs leaders who understand systems deeply, not just broadly.

Learning your position thoroughly does not mean staying forever. It means honoring the role enough to understand it before leaving it. Mastery includes knowing not only what works, but what fails and why. It includes leaving the position stronger than you found it. When you move forward with that level of understanding, you carry value with you rather than unfinished business.

Before transferring, ask yourself honest questions. Have I learned this role beyond the surface? Do I understand how my work affects others? Have I contributed meaningfully to the mission here? If the answer is yes, movement becomes progress. If the answer is no, movement becomes avoidance.

The goal in government service is not speed. It is readiness. Each position is a building block, not a stepping stone to be rushed across. When you take the time to learn before you leave, every transfer becomes an elevation rather than an escape. That discipline builds careers that last and agencies that function with strength and continuity.

47

When Being Helpful
Crosses into Being Used

G overnment service attracts people who care. Many public
servants take pride in stepping in, supporting coworkers,
and making sure the mission succeeds. That instinct to
help is one of the strengths of government work. But there is a line
sometimes thin, sometimes unnoticed between being helpful and
being used. When that line is crossed, both the individual and the
mission begin to suffer.

This threat connects to earlier discussions such as Taking on
More Than You Can Manage, Inability to Help Others with Their
Government Service, and Getting Others to Do Your Service Work
for You. Together, these ideas reveal a pattern. Some employees

consistently take on more than their share, while others quietly avoid responsibility. When those two behaviors coexist, imbalance becomes normalized. One person becomes overextended, while another becomes dependent on that generosity.

For many government employees, this shift happens gradually. It may start with helping a coworker who is learning or covering a task during a busy period. Over time, that assistance becomes expected. What began as support slowly turns into obligation. Coworkers and even supervisors begin to assume you will step in. Before long, you are carrying out responsibilities that are no longer temporary and no longer yours.

There are many reasons this happens. Some people fear disappointing others. Some believe that always saying yes will lead to recognition or advancement, a pattern discussed in Being Emotionally Dependent on Recognition. Others avoid setting boundaries because they want to be seen as dependable or cooperative. In some cases, coworkers intentionally shift their responsibilities onto whoever is willing to absorb them. Regardless of the cause, the outcome is the same. One employee becomes overloaded while another remains unchanged.

The cost of this imbalance is real. When you absorb too much work, the quality of your own service declines. Fatigue sets in. Resentment grows. Mistakes increase. Over time, even the most committed employee can begin to disengage. Ironically, trying to hold the mission together alone weakens the very system you are trying to protect.

Drawing boundaries is not selfish. It is professional. Being helpful should strengthen the mission, not quietly replace accountability. Every government position exists for a reason, and each workload is designed to be manageable by one person. When one employee consistently carries the work of multiple roles, it distorts expectations and prevents others from developing the skills they are responsible for learning.

Healthy boundaries also teach others how to serve. When you respectfully redirect a task back to its proper owner, you reinforce responsibility. You encourage growth rather than dependency. This is a quiet form of leadership. It aligns with the principles discussed in Ignoring the Opportunity to Lead Up to Supervisors. Accountability does not always come from authority. Sometimes it comes from clarity.

The key is balance. Help when it supports learning, teamwork, or temporary need. Step back when help becomes substitution. Protecting your energy and role allows you to serve consistently rather than burn out quietly.

Being helpful is one of the most admirable traits in government service. But helpfulness without boundaries becomes a liability. Knowing when to assist and when to step back ensures that your willingness to serve remains sustainable, respected, and effective. The mission does not need martyrs. It needs professionals who know how to give without disappearing in the process.

48

Treating Your Service Like a Job Instead of a Career

One of the most significant turning points in any government career is realizing that public service is more than employment; it is a career. Yet many government workers fall into the trap of treating their service as nothing more than a job. They come in, complete the bare minimum, and leave without a sense of craftsmanship, purpose, or pride. When this shift occurs, the quality-of-service declines, motivation fades, and the mission suffers.

This threat is deeply connected to several others in this book, including Failure to Understand What You Want to Give to Government Service, Having an Affinity for Government Failure, and Allowing Conflict and Shortcomings to Influence Your Commitment. Each reflects moments when the meaning behind the work begins to blur. But this chapter addresses something slightly different: what happens when a government employee stops seeing themselves as someone building a career at all.

A career demands discipline, development, and dedication to improvement. It requires understanding your role, owning your responsibilities, and caring about the outcomes you produce. Treating your service like a "job" removes those expectations. The mindset shifts from excellence to survival, from purpose to paycheck. Tasks become obligations rather than opportunities. Over time, the identity of a government employee erodes into someone who simply endures their work instead of shaping it.

This mentality rarely appears overnight. It often grows out of prolonged frustration, leadership turnover, internal conflict, or burnout. Sometimes it stems from hearing phrases like "it's just government work" repeated often enough to feel true. Whatever the cause, when employees disengage from the idea of building a career, standards quietly decline. Pride fades. Consistency weakens. And the public, who rely on government service daily, feel the impact.

The difference between a job and a career lies in ownership and intention. Someone building a career understands that their actions affect the credibility of the agency, the mission, and the community it serves. They recognize that their performance matters beyond supervision or evaluation. It matters because real people depend on the outcomes of government work for safety, stability, and opportunity.

A career mindset also requires growth. This connects directly to Refusal to Personally Invest in Your Own Career. Government service evolves, and those within it must evolve as well. Employees committed to their careers seek out learning opportunities, certifications, training, or education to remain effective. Even when development is not formally offered, they take initiative. They refuse to let their skills stagnate simply because the system moves slowly.

Treating your service as a career also changes how challenges are approached. People with a career mindset solve problems rather than avoid them. They communicate with purpose rather than complain. They prepare themselves for opportunity rather than waiting to be noticed. They hold themselves accountable not to avoid discipline, but because their standards demand it.

Perhaps most importantly, a career mindset defines how you show up when no one is watching. Recognition becomes secondary to integrity. The work is done well because it should be done well, not because praise is expected. This aligns with Being Emotionally Dependent on Recognition. Those committed to a career do not rely on applause to stay engaged. Their motivation is internal, steady, and durable.

Government agencies are strengthened when employees treat their service as a career rather than a job. Accountability improves. Collaboration becomes more intentional. Confidence in the mission grows, both internally and in the public eye. A workforce that thinks long-term builds systems that last.

Treat your service like a career because that is exactly what it is. Government work shapes lives, communities, and futures. When you approach your role with discipline, pride, and a commitment to growth, you are not just earning a paycheck. You are building something that carries weight, responsibility, and meaning over time.

49

Treating Neutrality as Harmless When It Is Not

Many government employees learn early how to survive within an agency. We learn about the culture quickly. We learn who speaks up and who stays quiet. We learn what topics bring consequences and which ones are safer to avoid. Over time, this often leads to a familiar strategy: keep a low profile, stay out of the way, and do your job without drawing attention. On the surface, neutrality can feel like professionalism. In reality, it can quietly become one of the most damaging positions a capable employee can take.

Neutrality in government is rarely neutral in effect. When employees who understand the work, see the problems, and know what could improve, choose silence, the mission does not pause. It continues forward without correction. Remaining neutral may protect your comfort, but it does not protect the public. This is where neutrality becomes harmful.

Government employees often believe they have three choices when confronted with dysfunction, inefficiency, or decline. They can actively push in the wrong direction. They can actively push in the right direction. Or they can stay neutral. Many choose neutrality because it appears safest. It avoids conflict with management. It avoids tension with coworkers. It avoids risk. But neutrality is still a decision. It is a decision to allow momentum to continue unchecked, even when that momentum leads away from effective service.

This threat connects closely with several others discussed throughout this book. In Ignoring the Opportunity to Lead Up to Supervisors, we explored how working staff often see problems long before leadership does. Choosing neutrality in those moments means surrendering one of your most valuable contributions. In Having an Affinity for Government Failure, we addressed the danger of disengaging emotionally from the mission. Neutrality often masks the same withdrawal, simply expressed more quietly. In Allowing Conflict and Shortcomings to Influence Your Commitment, we saw how frustration can lead employees to pull back instead of staying engaged. Neutrality is often the final stage of that retreat.

Some employees justify neutrality by saying they are not the cause of the problem. They may even believe they are acting responsibly by not interfering. But government service is not only about avoiding harm. It is about preventing it. When you understand the system and choose not to engage, you are still shaping outcomes. Silence allows poor practices to continue. Silence allows weak decisions to stand. Silence allows avoidable failures to repeat.

Staying neutral may keep you exactly where you are. It may protect your position, your schedule, and your sense of peace. But government service was never designed to be risk free. The public does not benefit from employees who simply avoid harm. They benefit from employees who apply judgment, experience, and care when it matters most.

Moving in the right direction does not require confrontation, ego, or control. It requires decision. It requires choosing to apply what you have learned throughout your career. It means using emotional intelligence when speaking up. It means leading up rather than lashing out. It means helping without overstepping and setting boundaries without disengaging. Neutrality avoids responsibility. Direction accepts it.

This threat is not about forcing every employee to become outspoken or confrontational. It is about recognizing that silence carries weight. When capable employees consistently choose neutrality, agencies stagnate. When neutrality becomes the norm, mediocrity feels acceptable and decline feels inevitable.

Government does not move forward on its own. It moves because people decide to move it. Remaining neutral may feel harmless in the moment, but over time it becomes permission for the mission to drift. The question is not whether neutrality keeps you safe. The question is whether it keeps the service honest, effective, and worthy of public trust.

At some point in every government career, neutrality stops being caution and starts becoming avoidance. When that moment arrives, a choice must be made. Stay still and protect yourself, or step forward and protect the mission. Only one of those choices truly serves the public. Which one will you choose?

50

Expecting Your Government Service to Fill Personal Voids

Having purpose in government service is powerful. It can motivate, inspire, and give us something meaningful to pour our time and energy into. But purpose is not the same thing as fulfillment. Too many government employees fall into the quiet trap of expecting their career to solve the emptiness, insecurities, or personal struggles they carry. Government service, at its core, is not designed to fill personal voids. It is designed to meet the needs of the public.

This threat connects deeply to many of the others described throughout this book, including Personal Agenda vs. Service Tasks, Approaching Your Service as "Owning Government," and Allowing Conflict and Shortcomings to Influence Your Commitment. In each of these, the common thread is the danger of merging personal needs with professional purpose. Government work can uplift you, but it cannot repair what must be healed internally.

This misunderstanding often begins innocently. Many of us enter government with pride and excitement, imagining that the service will become both our identity and our foundation. We romanticize the idea of being the helper, the protector, the problem solver. And during the good moments, this identity feels real and strong. But when the difficult moments arrive, and they always do, that same identity can feel shaken, threatened, or even broken.

Government work often exposes personal voids more than it heals them. The public's demands can be overwhelming. Internal politics can be draining. Leadership changes can disrupt stability. Conflicts, misunderstandings, mistakes, and unfairness can all cut deeper when the job is carrying emotional weight it was never meant to hold.

When the work becomes the source of confidence, self-worth, or identity, every challenge becomes personal. A denied request feels like rejection. A transfer feels like abandonment. Criticism feels like an emotional wound. Poor leadership feels like betrayal. This emotional dependency creates a cycle of frustration, instability, and disappointment that grows with every challenge.

The truth is simple, even if it is difficult to accept. Government service can add meaning to your life, but it cannot become your life. It can support you, but it cannot sustain you. It can strengthen you, but it cannot define who you are.

The parts of you that need healing, connection, belonging, or peace must be cared for outside the job. Family. Faith. Therapy. Community. Friendship. Personal interests. Rest. These are not distractions from service. They are what make healthy service possible.

When your personal life is grounded, something powerful happens at work. You approach challenges with clarity instead of emotion. You separate your identity from your assignment. You respond rather than react. You serve from strength rather than need. Your work becomes steadier, your judgment clearer, and your commitment more durable.

There is an important irony here. The less you expect government service to fill your personal voids, the more effective your service becomes. Your decisions are no longer driven by unmet needs. Your relationships are no longer strained by expectation. Your commitment becomes healthier because it is rooted in intention, not dependency.

Let the career be the career. Let your life be your life. The two can support each other, but neither should be asked to carry the full weight of the other. Government service is honorable and meaningful, but it is not a substitute for personal healing, connection, or wholeness.

As you close this book and return to your own path in government service, remember this. You were not hired to sacrifice yourself. You were hired to serve. Serve with clarity. Serve with balance. Serve from a place that is already supported by the things that truly sustain you.

And if you find yourself struggling, reach for help without shame. Employee assistance programs, human resources services, counselors, therapists, and trusted support systems exist because government employees are human first. Seeking help is not weakness. It is responsibility. Caring for yourself is not stepping away from service. It is how you remain capable of it.

Conclusion

Government service is not for the faint of heart. It is a career that demands patience, discipline, humility, and courage. It stretches you, challenges you, exposes your weaknesses, and strengthens your character. The work is rarely simple, often misunderstood, and sometimes deeply personal. The lessons come slowly, through experience, reflection, and at times real sacrifice. Yet those who remain committed to the mission, even through frustration and disappointment, are the ones who quietly shape the communities they serve.

The fifty threats outlined in this book are not meant to discourage you or burden you. They exist to inform, protect, and prepare you. Each threat represents a moment where direction can be lost, motivation can fade, or identity can become tangled in the system. But each one also represents a decision point. An opportunity to choose professionalism over resentment, growth over comfort, and purpose over disengagement.

Government work can feel heavy. It can feel confusing. At times, it can feel unfair. But it can also be meaningful, steady, and deeply rewarding when approached with clarity and intention. It is my hope that these reflections help you recognize the challenges without becoming defined by them, and that they strengthen your ability to remain grounded, resilient, and mission focused.

Never underestimate your role in the system. Your actions matter. Your integrity matters. Your decisions matter. Even when your effort feels invisible, the public experiences the results. Government is not an abstract idea. It is built daily through the choices of people like you. Every form processed, every conversation handled with care, every decision made with fairness contributes to the trust that the public places in the institutions meant to serve them.

Protect yourself as you serve. Guard your professionalism. Keep learning. Stay adaptable. Serve with intention rather than exhaustion. Remember that while the mission belongs to the public, the quality of that mission begins with the individuals entrusted to carry it forward.

If this book has accomplished anything, I hope it has reminded you that you are not alone. Every government employee encounters these threats in some form. What separates those who merely endure from those who truly serve is not the absence of obstacles, but the ability to navigate them with awareness, humility, and resolve.

Thank you for your service.

Thank you for your effort.

And thank you for choosing to remain committed to the mission, even when it tested you.